A WITCH IN MY HEART

A Witch in My Heart

A play set in Swaziland in the 1930s

HILDA KUPER

*Professor of Anthropology
in the University of California at Los Angeles
sometime Research Fellow of the International
African Institute*

with a Foreword by
MAX GLUCKMAN

*Professor of Social Anthropology
in the University of Manchester*

Published for the
INTERNATIONAL AFRICAN INSTITUTE
by the
OXFORD UNIVERSITY PRESS, LONDON
1970

Oxford University Press, Ely House, London W. 1

GLASGOW NEW YORK TORONTO MELBOURNE WELLINGTON
CAPE TOWN SALISBURY IBADAN NAIROBI DAR ES SALAAM LUSAKA ADDIS ABABA
BOMBAY CALCUTTA MADRAS KARACHI LAHORE DACCA
KUALA LUMPUR SINGAPORE HONG KONG TOKYO

SBN 19 724180 8

Typeset by
H. Charlesworth & Co. Ltd.
and
printed in Great Britain by
Lowe and Brydone

CONTENTS

It is a privilege to introduce this play of Hilda Kuper's about how a favourite, but barren, wife, is accused of witchcraft, and feels in her own heart she may be guilty. But I feel it it somewhat impertinent for me to do so, since she and I began our studies in social anthropology in the same class on the same day. I do so, however, because it was I who urged on her that the play had lain too long unpublished; and that if she were to write an introduction analysing the position of women in Swazi society in the 1930's, the whole would make an important contribution to our understanding of life in Africa. It is not only I who think thus of the play: the Swazi themselves have reacted similarly. The play was written in English but translated into Zulu which is closely related to Swazi and is the language used in Swazi schools. Under the title *Inhliziyo Ngumthakathi* it was published by Shuter and Shooter in Natal, South Africa. The Swazi educational authorities accepted the play and it has become a standard textbook in Swazi schools. Swazi authorities consider it an authentic and dramatic presentation of a situation in which a woman is accused of witchcraft and of the misery that results. The play was first performed by African students at the University of Natal.

For non-Swazi, the play's dramatic quality is marked; and as I studied the Zulu, neighbours of the Swazi, who in family organisation are much akin, I can vouch for its ethnographic authenticity.

Social anthropologists collect material and experiences which may be handled in scientific terms, or treated dramatically in story. Few of them can do both. Hilda Kuper is one of these talented few. Her high standing as a social anthropologist, with her present position as Professor of Anthropology in the University of California at Los Angeles, is based on solid contributions to science, notabley: *An African Aristocracy: Rank among the Swazi of Swaziland* (1947), *The Uniform of Colour: A Study of White-Black Relationships in Swaziland* (1947), and *Indian People in Natal* (1960), as well as her editorship of *Urbanization and*

Migration in West Africa (1965) and (with L. Kuper) of *African Law: Adaptation and Development* (1965). She has also written many articles published in scientific journals. At the same time there appeared in literary journals a number of her short stories about Swazi both in their homeland and at work in the towns of South Africa, and in 1966 her novel *Bite of Hunger* set in Swaziland of the 1930's was published in America and in England.

I have felt that this present play should be published both for its own dramatic merit, and for the vividness with which it brings out the shape of common human dilemmas within Swazi culture. But I also have a special reason for urging her to consent to its publication. When social anthropologists analyse the setting of accusations of witchcraft, they bring out the extent to which this type of belief is associated with a certain stage of economic and social development — in Europe's past as in Africa. They concentrate on what might be called the 'functional significance' of the beliefs and the accusations that flow from the beliefs. One of my students said that when he was ultimately confronted with witchcraft in his research he was horrified to find that its actuality was so miserable: he had thought of it as serving society. But no anthropologist has baulked the fact that to live in a situation where the agony of misfortune, illness or death, is aggravated by the fear that you may have suffered because of the evil machinations of someone close to you (brother, or wife, sister, uncle or nephew, depending on the social organisation of the people concerned) is miserable and agonising. The distressed reaction of all human beings to misfortune is made worse by such beliefs, arising from social and economic conditions which have been analysed repeatedly. Whatever the miseries of industriali-zation, it has liberated us, and will liberate Africans, from adding to our misfortunes the fear that they are caused by the alleged occult powers of those we love.

University of Manchester   Max Gluckman
31 August, 1969.

INTRODUCTION

When I wrote *A Witch in My Heart* I was not trying, at least at the conscious level, to interpret a specific situation as an anthropologist. To me the situation was less about witchcraft and more about the heart — a symbolic heart reflecting deep human emotions — love, hate, jealousy, hope, and despair. It happened that the people about whom I wrote were Swazi, and among them these emotions were expressed in a particular cultural idiom in which witchcraft was an essential and accepted element, a part of the general order and disorder of life.

In literature perhaps more than in any other field we are able to contemplate the problem of the relationship between the universal and the particular. The human body is much the same the world over — longer or shorter, more or less hairy, darker or lighter. The basic structure and functions demarcated by sex persist through reproduction. But these basic biological universals merely stake the boundaries of mankind in a vast physical universe. They do not answer the complex emotional questions posed by the demands of human biology nor do they produce a common language of ideas. By what compounding of experiences, in what perplexities of situations, is a human body transformed into a person, an individual, social and yet unique?

Anthropologists concerned with formalized social relations, discuss the general rather than the particular, the usual rather than the exceptional, *'the'* person rather than *'a'* person; and interpret their 'findings' in the context of theories and assumptions developed in particular schools within the discipline. Students are then trained to handle as their tools a selected range of methodo-logical and analytical principles and the requisite professional vocabulary. Everyday words are necessarily defined and re-defined by each disciple in the esoteric circle; people and situations are reduced in technical, professional language to norms, formulae, and figures.

An anthropologist who has lived closely with people in foreign lands is confronted with the very difficult problem of how to present her data. To communicate with her colleagues she must fit her material, expressed in a world of different symbols, into the compartments acceptable in the discipline. She is expected to write in scientific journals and monographs, aware of problems of social rather than personal relationships. No matter how deeply her experiences and reflections in the 'field' change her perceptions and enrich her personal life, she must strive to be 'objective' by the standards of her colleagues in the craft.

The writer of fiction, on the other hand, is allowed greater freedom of expression and imagination. She is expected to personalize general experiences, is permitted to develop her own style and eccentricities, and encouraged to avoid technical formulations and conventions in making her own commitments. Her ideas may change without the criticism of inconsistency and her characters can express contradictions without evoking acrimonious reviews by scholars of other schools. She need not explicitly distinguish between ideas and emotions and may deliberately use the ambiguity of words to extend the reader's perception. Since she does not have to prove 'facts' or test hypotheses she may allow vision to replace 'reality.' Her history need not be chronological nor social, nor her cosmology computable. She may take for granted that the mind sets its own pace as it wanders through an existential labyrinth. She is permitted to *be* the blind sage of the Dogon without attempting to justify his existence. She is entitled to ecstasy:

> 'To find eternity in a grain of sand and heaven
>   in a wild flower.
> To hold the world in the palm of the hand and
>   infinity in an hour.'

But because the artist as well as the anthropologist or any other being is part of the world in which she lives, she remains partly grounded by the conventions of that world. It marks and limits her imagination so that even the world of creation is never completely culture free and boundless. At the same time the 'discoveries' of anthropologists, as well as of astronauts and other adventurers, have already extended the horizon of writers of fiction, and provided artists with new insights and new imagery.

The drama, the novel, the poem, and the monograph complement one another, each presenting a different facet of the whirling worlds around and within the self.

My play is set in Swaziland — a lovely little country in South-East Africa — before the winds of change stirred colonial dust into the storms of independence. At that time, which I consider here as the historic present, Swaziland, despite over forty years of British rule, is isolated from the outside world of industry and commerce. The Swazi people who constitute the majority of the population live at a low subsistence level, cultivating crops and tending cattle. As a consequence of a concession period, a small minority of whites still own nearly two-thirds of the country, and so-called 'Swazi Areas' are scattered in between large European-owned farms. When money is required for tax and a limited range of new essentials, Swazi men seek work with whites as temporary unskilled migrant labourers. Wages are generally low, and, particularly on the farms, living conditions are often poor; so most Swazi prefer to go for varying periods to the towns and mines of the Union (now the Republic) of South Africa. They return if possible for the ploughing season, to resume their life with their families on the land.

Acquiescence is not acceptance, and while the Swazi submit to colonial domination, they do not accept it as right, and they deliberately maintain many of their own traditions. They pay their tax in money to 'chiefs of the office' (officials of the white government) but give their deeper loyalty to 'chiefs of the people' and above all to their own hereditary King, the Ngwenyama, Lion, who shares his power with his mother, the Ndlovukati, Lady Elephant.

The rulers live in villages of some hundred people, but most Swazi, aristocrats and commoners, live in isolated homesteads close to the fields they cultivate. Each homestead is under a headman who has the right to decide who should, and who may, stay in his domain. His rank, determined by pedigree, and wealth, influences the size and compositon of the homestead, but it is rare to find a homestead occupied by a single elementary family remote from close kin. Describing the ideal homestead, informants say, 'There should always be a headman with his mother, his wives and his children. And it is best if there are also his brothers and their families, and the wives and children of their sons.' The homestead thus is essentially a patriarchal, patrilocal establishment with a bias to polygyny.

Each woman together with her own children forms a distinct economic and social group. They have their own share of the estate – a cluster of huts enclosed in a high reed fence, their own gardens for cultivation, and their special allocation of cattle. When there is too little land, or friction occurs between the inhabitants, the headman sanctions separation along clearly existing lines – mothers with their married sons and unmarried children move away. They retain their legal and economic interests in the general estate but are spared the strain of most intimate face to face contacts.

Swazi say, 'Polygyny is the nature of man; a woman fulfils herself through children.' A dilemma is involved in both these notions: the boundaries of the structure in which these notions are held are fixed, but the operational limits of each are open to divergent and individual interpretations. Polygyny is built into the system of politics, law, economics, and ritual, but there is no definition of whether the 'nature of man' requires two, ten, or twenty wives. Again, children are the most valued social possession, but the desired number is not specified. Polygyny does not permit a man to accumulate women indiscriminately nor is a woman encouraged to reproduce indefinitely. Discussions with Swazi friends showed that polygyny was never confused with promiscuity; the former was a question of rank, the latter of sexuality. Sexuality is fleeting fun, rank an enduring responsibility. If a man goes beyond his rank, he runs the risk of incurring the enmity of men whose position he is challenging and of those who feel deprived by his excesses.

The number of children a woman bears is complicated by the uncontrollable element of 'luck or 'fortune' (*intlantla*) An unmarried girl is expected to take lovers, but condemned if she conceives. After she has been received as wife, the bearing of children is an essential duty. The number of children a married woman bears is also limited by social factors, including a prohibition on full intercourse during a long period of suckling – a prohibition which carries the sanction that the life of the older infant would be endangered. Miscarriages are frequent and infant mortality very high, and during the months of mourning, intercourse with a bereaved mother is also taboo. In response to the question 'how many children have you', the dead as well as the living are always mentioned. From the genealogies I collected it seems that very few women have more than four grown-up children. The general opinion seems to be expressed in the statement that 'to have no child is death (*khufa*), to have only one child is dangerous (or risky – *ingoti*), but ten is frightening (*kuyesabekha*).

Swazi society is relatively unspecialized and the people who live together co-operate closely in work, worship, and recreation. The system of kinship classification embraces within a single term a number of people who in more specialized societies are kept distinct. Thus the term *babe* (father) is extended from a specific male to his brothers, half brothers, and sons of his father's brothers, and on the same principle *make* includes 'the woman who bore me,' her sisters, wives of my father's brothers and all my mother's co-wives. Each inclusive term serves as a mnemonic, reminding a person with whom she – or he – may eat, sleep, or joke; who must give and who may take; who must be respected and who avoided. Implicit in the system is the assumption that people covered by the same term share for certain purposes a common social identity.

In the homestead we can observe the many-faceted relationships of male and female, which is the major dichotomy of life, through the roles of husband and wife, father and mother, son and daughter, brother and sister, and the homologous in-law structure — father-in-law, mother-in-law, child-in-law of either sex. The roles which are imposed on a single person simultaneously, sometimes support and sometimes contradict one another, creating the dilemma of choice of alignment, a dilemma particularly acute for a woman.

Children of both sexes are desired, but because of the total social structure a son is more essential for women as well as men. A woman must not live in the home of a married daughter — a separation rationalised by the difficulties in which it would place her husband in his dual role of headman with its associated authority, and of son-in-law with its demand that he must show 'shame' before his mother-in-law. But a woman *should* live in the home of her married son where, irrespective of her personal qualities, she is given a position of honour and power, and controls and instructs her son's wives and their children, and sees that her son does not neglect his duties as husband or father.

Mother and son are key symbols in Swazi culture. Like all symbols, they stand for many and often opposed values and ideas at different levels. 'Mother' is woman, reproduction, earth, soft rain; but 'woman' is also dangerous, polluting and disruptive. The 'son' is masculinity ('the bull,' strength, responsibility, 'the pole of the hut'); as man he is also lightning and war. A wife as woman has the power to create but she also has the power to withold creation. Sterility is always blamed on the woman. If there are no children a homestead dies as surely as, and more fearfully than, if destroyed in open battle.

Marriage, a lengthy process, is legally validated by the transfer of property (*ukulobola*) between two groups — the one that gives a girl and receives cattle, the other that gives cattle and receives a girl. The group that gives the cattle obtains exclusive rights over any children the woman may bear, even after the death of the husband. The emotions of the individuals are relatively unimportant.

But while relationships may be defined by transfer of property,

xiv

that which is created are relationships between people, not between things or even people and things. Property, including cattle, cannot make human claims. Although it might appear as if women are at times equated with cattle, they have their own well-defined and recognized rights and powers.

The rank of wives is not equal. It varies with a number of principles — pedigree, seniority, mode of marriage. A man's first wife should be selected for him by his father, who provides the marriage payment to her parents. Described as 'wiper away of his boyhood darkness' she shares some of the responsibilities and privileges of a man's mother, but is never automatically appointed the principal wife, mother of the 'eater of the inheritance.' Some wives have *tinhlanti* (plur.) — subordinate co-wives provided by principles stated explicitly in the rules of kinship relationships. A woman and her sisters are closely identified, and the most usual *inhlanti* (sing.) is a full junior sister, or the daughter of a mother's brother since it is he who benefitted by his sister's marriage cattle. The older woman is the Big Wife, and the children of the junior (Little) wife will, for all legal purposes, be considered as her own. Swazi phrase many relationships in the language of marriage payments and for the junior wife only a single additional beast need be given.

When a headman dies the choice of successor is made by his family council (*lusendvo*) which evaluates not the sons of the deceased but his widows as 'mothers.' The council consists of senior members of his agnatic lineage together with his own oldest sister and his own mother or mother surrogate. They take into consideration the clan of each woman, previous marriage links in terms of preferential marriages, between kinsfolk, and ultimately the character of the woman. A woman whose marriage was arranged by elders of the lineage is far more likely to be appointed than one who made love for herself (*watiganela*). Individual passion as a basis for marriage is treated as a destructive element in a society regulated by rights of larger units of kin. So important are the lineage affiliations of a woman in the choice of a man's heir, that should she be childless but obviously of the highest rank, a child of another wife (preferably her own sister) will be 'put into her stomach' i.e., be given her as her own and be the main heir. From the public viewpoint this is an effective adjustment to a situation resulting from the inability of the barren woman to fulfil a legal contract, as well as social duty, for which her lineage as a whole is responsible. But, and Swazi recognize this too, from the viewpoint of the women directly and personally involved, the arrangement is ambiguous and difficult, and often tense. Even though the older woman was consulted, and the younger woman consented, to be 'the rafter' to the house, there are predictable currents of hostility. The older wife may fear that her husband's affection will be alienated by the younger woman especially once she gives him children, and the younger woman may deeply resent not only her own subordinate status but the claim exercised by the older, privately as well as publicly, over the 'rafter's' children. The children themselves, despite the verbalised theory of equality of 'mothers,' may indicate more positive affection for 'the mother who bore me and suckled me,' even though they derive their economic benefits from the status of the older barren 'mother.'

The Swazi emphasize that a woman's major role is not that of wife but of mother. The situation is expressed in a riddle formulated from the male standpoint: 'If your mother and wife were drowning, whom would you save?' The correct answer is; 'My mother; I can get another wife, (but not another mother).' The more rarely formulated counterpart from the woman's side, 'If your husband and child were drowning, whom would you save?' does not draw the response 'My husband, because I cannot get another' or 'because he can make me another child' but, 'My child, because he was borne by me.'

Within the homestead, the rules of descent and residence give prominence to the headman's agnatic kin; but the perpetuation and expansion of his line depend on the women they marry. This reveals the paradoxical situation, found in many patrilineal polygynous societies, in which property and power are inherited from men and acquired by men, but are transmitted through women who are brought in as 'outsiders' to the men's group. Males increase the depth of a single lineage; women as mothers are the nodes at which it multiplies and divides. Swazi draw an analogy with the pumpkin plant. 'A pumpkin plant dies before the pumpkin.' The pumpkin bears both male and female flowers on the same vine. The plant is 'the mother.' When the pumpkins ripen, the plant dies. The pumpkins are the 'sons.' They carry the seeds that will produce other vines and other flowers, both female and male.

A woman on marriage leaves the protection of her own kin but is never fully incorporated into the homestead of her husband or identified with his lineage. She retains her father's clan name, which is different from that of her husband and her children, and throughout her married life her conduct is regulated by special rules of *hlonipha* (from *inhloni* — shame, respect) expressed in a complex of prohibitions and avoidances.

Wives, particulary young wives, are conspicuous outsiders in the homestead of their common husband, set apart by clothing, movements, gestures, and speech from 'the calves of the home' — the daughters and sisters of the headman. The contrast between the two sets of alignments — affinal and natal — is dramatically expressed at different points in the elaborate process of marriage. A bride, before she leaves her natal home, is counselled by her parents on how to endure the trials of wifehood. Her mother, weeping, instructs her to comport herself with humility and restraint though she be insulted and even accused of witchcraft. On the marriage morning she stands in the cattle byre of her in-laws lamenting in song the loss of her girlhood freedom and appeals to her 'brothers' to come and rescue her. These men, representing her own people, have been waiting in hiding. They respond with loud shouts of aggression against the man's group and rush off with their girl in their midst. But she knows, and they know, that she must finally accept the role of woman as wife and she returns, docile but unsmiling, when her future mother-in-law calls her back with the promise of a cow. Later, a child from her husband's group is placed on her lap, representing directly the main purpose for which she has been taken as wife. After this she ceremonially distributes gifts brought from her home to the various in-laws whose goodwill is so necessary for her future happiness.

As an in-law she must wear the heavy skin skirt of marriage; she must not eat certain foods, including milk of her husband's cattle; she must go around and not in front of the shrine hut associated with his lineage; and, most pervasive of the avoidance rules, she must learn a new and more restricted language, a language of circumlocution which avoids the use of the names or words similar to the first syllable of the names of the senior male in-laws.

This complex of avoidances, some indirect and subtle, some crude and obvious, provide a barrier of exclusion enforced against every married woman by every other member of the homestead. If a young wife transgresses (*ukona*) by deed or word, she must 'show shame' and beg forgiveness. If she persists the elders say her tongue will rot or she will be punished in some other horrible way by wrathful ancestors. There is no need for legal intervention and though informants say a fine could be demanded from her family, no single case could be cited. Some of the restrictions demarcating the exclusion are removed when the wife becomes a mother and mother-in-law.

Unlike other situations in which 'outsiders' unite or conspire against an in-group, the exclusion from the husband's line does not lead to the formation of an opposition organization of co-wives. Co-wives are described by others as 'the wives of such-and-such a man' and in many situations such as marriages, deaths, and illnesses are treated as a single unit, but they have no permanent and enduring ties with one another. They are involved in many co-operative domestic activities, but their fragmentation is reflected in the fact that each woman retains her own clan name on marriage or is known as the 'mother of so-and-so' — the name of her own children by the common husband.

The danger of friction within this somewhat miscellaneous collection of women is recognized. A special term, *bukhwele* (from *kukhwela-* to climb), is applied to the rivalry and jealousy of co-wives; it is a potentially disruptive reaction of all women as wives. A man has a very intimate relationship with all his wives' sisters (his *balamu*) and in Swazi theory, 'the love of sisters overcomes the jealousy of co-wives.' But Swazi also are well aware that in fact each wife, whether independent or subordinate, related or unrelated, is an individual competing for the same scarce resource – the favour of the man. All co-wives, related or not, address each other as 'sister.' The provision of a junior co-wife serves the interests of the groups bound by the marriage payment but may conflict with the personal desires of individuals.

A polygynist's lot is not an easy one. When he has brought a new wife into the harem he must do all he can not to awaken jealousy by showing her special preference in the garden lands that he allots, in the clothes that he gives her, or the time he spends in her company. The man, who has his own hut to which he calls his wives, should be careful to spend his time equally between them. There are predictable tensions and cleavages in a homestead in which there is a barren woman who is the favourite of her husband and a young pregnant wife who is afraid of labour pains and of the envious disposition of the barren woman.

Divorce is rare and difficult to obtain, especially for a woman. A man and his lineage have different rights (and interests) in her as wife and as mother. A man has exclusive sexual rights in his wife during his lifetime; his agnates have enduring rights in her productivity as a mother. Polygyny, which sanctions a double standard of morality, permits a man who is sexually dissatisfied with a wife to pursue unmarried women and bring them to his home; a wife has no such freedom. Formerly, if caught *in flagrante delicto*, the woman and her lover could be killed; under colonial law the husband has the right to exact a heavy fine from the 'thief' and either thrash the erring wife or send her back to her own kin. A husband has the right to beat a wife for a number of faults, though he may himself be fined if he 'breaks the skin.'

A man, as husband, is involved with a woman in the most intimate aspects of marriage and as long as she pleases him as a wife, is not an econimc burden, and is faithful to him, he is generally prepared to keep her even though she is barren. His agnates, who contributed to the marriage payment, and have invested in her fertility, do not benefit by her personal services, and are more prepared to tolerate infidelity than barrenness. If she has no progeny after several years of marriage they may insist on her kin providing her with a junior co-wife or demand recovery of their property through the court.

The expulsion of a woman by her husband or affines is a serious insult which may have disruptive repercussions in the homesteads of her own agnatic kin. If the man's group claims redress in the courts by making open allegations against her for misbehaviour or failure to fulfil recognised obligations, her people will defend her publicly and try to have her reinstated. However, if she is ordered to 'tie her luggage and go,' but there is no mention of claiming return of marriage payment, the position of the woman and her kin is more ambivalent. Under colonial law it is illegal publicly to proclaim a person a witch; however for a person in authority, especially a father-in-law, to expel a woman from his home without laying any formal charge against her, indicates that he has adequate evidence against her as a witch even though no open accusation be made.

Because the cattle given for a woman are used to obtain wives by her own agnates, more especially by a full brother, she is legally as well as morally entitled to claim protection and support from him if necessary, and she holds a privileged position in his home. The wives, her sisters-in-law, must treat her with the greatest deference and should never refuse her any reasonable requests. But if she is rejected by her husband and returns permanently to her natal home, she becomes a threat to their own security. If the marriage cattle are claimed back as a result of a law suit, their husband may be put into an awkward economic difficulty, but if the dismissal is based on divination even though no cattle are claimed, they may believe that their well-being, indeed their very lives, are threatened.

I have heard of no cases in which a husband was accused of using witchcraft against his wives — but in several cases wives have suspected a sister-in-law, and have shouted this at her in bitterness. But they know that the husband — the 'witch's' kin — is unlikely to agree with this accusation for it reflects on him as well. A married woman who visits her brother with her husband's permission is a 'princess of the home' a 'calf of her people,' but a woman who comes to live there permanently, especially if she has been rejected by her husband, carries the taint and power of witchcraft with her, and is a source of hatred and of fear. For her, as well as for the wives as sisters-in-law, this is an insoluble and at times tragic dilemma.

'To have no child is the greatest pain.' Barrenness is both a misfortune and a danger. The barren woman is unfortunate because she may have been bewitched; she is a danger because in her envy she may bewitch a fertile wife and her children.

To deal with the hazards of life that range from failure of crops to barren women, Swazi apply a set of notions and techniques that are especially expressed through the ancestral cult, the vital religion of the people, and through an elaborate system of magic. No Swazi would ever boast 'I am the master of my fate.' He *knows* that outside man are forces (non-material and spiritual) greater than man.

The Swazi dogma of conception states that coitus is required to 'make a child,' but over and above the sexual act itself is the power of the deities to bestow the miracle of creation on a limited number of such acts. Barrenness, in the first place, is generally interpreted as a sign of displeasure of the ancestors. If a woman does not conceive within the first year of marriage, the in-laws may make offerings to their ancestors and similar appeal may be made at the home of the girl by her father or, if he is dead, by her brother. When these appeals are not successful they will con-

sult various specialists, seeking cause and cure. But there is never th
assumption that the cure will be effected by medicines alone.

The ancestors punish descendants who ignore familial obligations, more especially who neglect 'to remember' their forefathers in offerings and sacrifice. Sometimes even though they
have blessed a marriage with conception they exert their power
at the point of delivery, making labour difficult and further
sacrifice essential. If the woman is still unable to produce the
child, she may be accused of adultery and urged to confess in
order that the necessary purification can take place and the child
be accepted by its mother's husband as father or *pater*, and hence
by his lineage.

In a polygynous homestead, a barren woman may become the
focus of the deepest tensions and fears and antagonisms. The
children of other wives are proof of the man's virility and
fertility. The childless woman is incomplete, abnormal — a thing
to pity, scorn or fear. When all is well (with all but the unfortunat
co-wives may treat her kindly, encouraging their own children to
give her help when necessary, to smear the floors of her hut,
bring her water and wood, and sometimes grind grain for the
daily meal or cook for her. But as soon as there is misfortune,
more especially if a child of a co-wife falls ill or dies, she is
vulnerable to subtle ostracism, suspicion, and even open hatred
and aggression. Her danger is intensified if the shared husband
shows her particular attention.

The world of the ancestors is a static replication of that of the
living, and, as on earth, kinship provides the boundaries of most
meaningful relationships. The agnatic ancestors have a strong
disciplinary aspect carrying into the religious system the basic
form of authority of the parental over the filial generation developed in the domestic domain. Structurally, the responsibility for
the ancestral cult rests with those in the subordinate (filial)
status. No act is more heinous than for a son to raise his hand
against his father; but for a father to inflict punishment demon-
strates his legitimate authority.

The agnatic ancestors of man and woman have complementary and at times conflicting roles. Those of the man are more concerned with maintaining authority and with the birth of a healthy child than with the well-being of the mother. The woman's ancestors are more concerned with her interests as *their* child, and are less formal and more protective.

Illness and other misfortunes are frequently attributed to ancestors (*emadloti*) per se but Swazi believe that no ancestors inflict suffering through malice, wanton cruelty or evil. It is as custodians of correct familial behaviour that they punish directly or vicariously the mean husband, the adulterous wife, the over-ambitious younger brother, the disobedient son. Though the ancestors punish, they do not wish to destroy. As part of the continuing life of a lineage they too desire health, prosperity, and children. Between the ethics of the ancestors and the mundane desires of their living descendants there is no conflict. Swazi desire the ends they say the ancestors desire for them. Even the man's agnatic ancestors, dependent as they are for their survival on the memorial services conducted by their descendants, have an interest in the wives who bear those descendants. They do not destroy even transgressing wives who are their daughters-in-law.

The ancestors are more powerful and wiser than the living, but they are not omnipotent; they are one of a number of occult agencies which can explain failure, unhappiness, misfortune and death.

Logically supporting the cult of the ancestors are beliefs in witch-craft, an evil destructive power, exercised by living men and women in the circle of their own acquaintances. Some African peoples distinguish between witches with an inherent physiological propensity to evil and sorcerers who use medicines and are consciously, deliberately evil. Among the Swazi the same term (*abatsakatsi*) is applied to all techniques though the evil power may be used in different ways.

In this patrilineal society the power of witchcraft is believed to be generally transmitted through the woman, the outsider, and not through the father to his children. The witch mother inoculates one or all of her children with *butsakatsi* when the child is still at the breast. This initial inoculation, however, is not sufficient to convert a normal human being into a witch. The witch potentiality must receive direction and training; the young witch is gradually introduced into the foul society of witches and buys its final acceptance with the destruction of somebody dear and of the same flesh and blood. A woman whose children die for no apparent reason or who has frequent miscarriages or is barren may in some circumstances be pitied as a victim of witchcraft, and in others be feared as a witch.

Death is the ultimate weapon of witches, and witchcraft itself is a crime punishable with banishment or death; to accuse some-one of being a witch thus carries a serious responsibility.

A witch cannot be discovered by the ordinary process of law based on open questions and visible evidence. She can only be detected by an equally powerful occult or esoteric agent. For this purpose Swazi consult diviners. Swazi diviners employ a wide range of techniques, one of the most common being that described in this play but there are other oracular devices that serve the same purpose: in all cases the decision is made by a supposedly impartial inspired outsider or by a supposedly neutral instrument. Thereby the responsibility of pronouncing a person a witch is not placed on the consultants who initiate the procedure and/or who are involved as sufferers. They believe in all good faith that they simply provide the medium (diviner or oracle) with the facts *as they know them*. The description of divination in the play is simplified for dramatic effect.

Diviners are men of considerable intelligence; they are not charlatans. Some in their techniques demand a response from their consultants, others operate without any external aids. Consultants may go to more than one diviner, reluctant to face the disruptive consequences of pointing out a witch. The fact that several diviners in different places and without contact between them confirm one another's findings, reinforces the belief in their impartiality and provides the necessary legitimacy and morality for subsequent action. The sentence is just in accordance with the verdict of divination.

The relationships involved in situations of witchcraft are of a different social order from those which emerge from the examination of reports of ordinary murders in western society or those reconstructed in 'who done it' mystery novels. In these, even if the murder were not premeditated, the relationship between victim and murderer is essentially personal and direct. In witchcraft there are certain structural cleavages which involve a number of people who need not be consciously aware of their actions or in direct contact with each other. Confronted with the corpse, they may not know that they are guilty until they are told why they committed the crime. The death of a new-born child is particularly revealing — the real murderer must be traced through the network of kinship in which a child is a crucial but vulnerable link. Its sudden death may be due to a long chain of events stretching back to the period before its mother was even taken as a wife.

The real cause is associated with motives, and motives are embedded in relationships over different periods of time and in many circumstances. The concern of those who want to discover the witch is less with the dead than with the living, and less with the present than with the past and future. (In the play, when Bigwapi's co-wives express to one another their suspicion that she is a witch, they recall with fear her background, before she married Sikova, and how she reacted, as well as her behaviour in his homestead, her self-imposed isolation, the excuses she made to avoid being with them, and what she said on different occasions.) A highly intelligent herbalist, with a reputation of knowledge of witchcraft, once said to me in English, 'As you know, Professor, you have to probe old wounds to prevent new infections.'

Accusations of witchcraft thus bring to the surface the undercurrents of tensions and suspicions, but their significance goes beyond the superficial level of interpersonal antagonisms. It is not the wife whose child died who goes to consult a diviner, but her father-in-law. The information he feeds to the diviner is couched unwittingly in terms of his own position in the kinship network and hence his own perceptions of the case.

Witchcraft accusations have been analysed in terms of four key positions: accuser, victim, medium, and accused. The situation however, is even more complex for each of these postions may itself include persons with diverse kinship orientations. The accuser is not necessarily the person who has been ill, nor is it necessarily the victim who dies; witchcraft is suffered as well as practised vicariously. The deepest injury may be through the surviving self – the mother is 'killed' through her child, the lover through the death of the beloved. Moreover, and more significantly, the accuser does not necessarily represent the interests of those whose cause he is espousing. The selection of a witch is, unconsciously guided by each person's view of his or her relationship with others in the broader social structure of the society.

The headman consults the diviner, ostensibly on behalf of all his dependants, but he as well as each of them has his or her own complex of rights and interests in the accused. As a father, and father-in-law, he may be justified in banishing a son's favourite wife as a witch; the son, as husband, may have no desire to accept this verdict, but as son he has no alternative. Bound by his culture he does not perceive that had he been the consultant she would not have been the accused. Since the role of son takes precedence over that of husband, he must abide by the decision given by the diviners to his father.

His mother may pity both the woman and her son, but as a wife she is legally subordinate to her husband, and powerless to change or challenge the verdict. She could protect her daughter-in-law from her son as husband, but not from her husband as father-in-law.

The accused barren wife is the focus of the most tragic conflict between different legal rules intensified by personal emotions. She stands alone, an outsider without the only justification – children – that will entitle her to permanent admission in her

usband's home. Yet if she returns without permission to her
wn kin she is rejected by them as well. Her dilemma is more
nsoluble if she has exceptional talents — such as special skill in
rt, or the gift that we ourselves call 'green fingers,' or a creativity
n words, or any power to captivate.

The external enemies of a witch are motivated by envy, hatred,
nd malice; but within herself are the qualities that lead to her
destruction. The enemies, organised into different categories
ccording to their particular interests, confront her in all her
omplex and contradictory roles as a single person — 'the witch.'

The play deals with the fate of a barren woman in a society
which accepts polygyny as an ideal, considers children the fulfil-
ment of womanhood, and believes in witchcraft. It is the drama of
particular woman, not of all barren women in the society. In the
ituation there is a ruthless logic but no universal inevitability.

The main characters of the play are members of the homestead
of the headman, Ntamo Zwane, and the relationship between
hem is shown on the accompanying chart.

In the course of his long life, Zwane had several wives, but only
ne, NaboSikova (Mother of Sikova), is still alive. Sikova himself
lready has three wives, two of them sisters, the Big and the Little
Hlope, Hlope being the clan name of their father. The third wife is
he beautiful, exceptional Bigwapi. The Big Hlope had a son who
died in infancy and she now has only a small daughter, Tekani.
The Little Hlope is pregnant. Bigwapi, though married before her
nd in spite of treatment from many doctors is still childless.

When Bigwapi's younger sister, Lomusa, comes on a visit Ntamo
uggests to Sikova that he take her as Bigwapi's subordinate co-
wife (*inhlanti*) to bear children. For her, a wife's younger sister,
only token marriage payment would be required. Sikova rejects
he idea on the grounds that three wives are as many as he desires
or can afford. Ntamo argues that Sikova has not three wives since
a barren woman does not count as a wife.

Though the relationship between Bigwapi and Lomusa is very
close, Bigwapi is not eager to have Lomusa as an additional wife,

and Lomusa herself finds Sikova's friend, Jobeni, more desirable. Bigwapi is still hopeful that her barrenness will be cured and that it will not be necessary for her to share her husband with her own sister as well as with the two Hlope girls.

Medical treatment, however, is expensive, and Sikova, responsive to Bigwapi's reactions, decides that he will go to Johannesburg, the 'Place of Gold,' to earn the necessary money. He asks permission from his parents and they agree reluctantly, insisting only that he does not work in the mines, where his older brother was killed.

Sikova experiences the city as hostile and frightening. He is not able to find the relative with whom he was to live, but is lucky to be befriended by 'a Swazi from a white man's farm,' who produces the necessary 'references,' gets him a job, and introduces him to his shebeen (drinking-shop) friends. While he is with them, he receives a letter telling him that his new baby has died and that he must go home. He sits stunned, a glass of brandy in his hand. The place is raided by the police and he is taken to gaol.

In the meantime his father goes to consult diviners to find the 'true cause' of the death. He learns what he suspected — Bigwapi is the witch. In spite of her protests and her tears he banishes her from his home 'before she commits any further evil.'

Sikova, on his release from prison, vows that he will discover the witch who killed his child and will wreak just vengeance. He has no idea who it may be and cries in bewilderment. 'Who could hate me so?' When he returns to find 'the home' of which he dreamed 'has turned into a grave,' and is told that his beloved, Bigwapi, is the witch, he cannot at first believe this, yet he cannot doubt that 'truth' is revealed by divination. As a son he finally accepts his father's action in executing the diviner's verdict.

The tragic irony of this situation is accentuated by the fact that when Sikova accepts the decision he is not able to continue the obligation by which it was justified. The depersonalised pronouncement destroys all Sikova's closest ties. Sikova, as the son, cannot take back his witch, his dearest wife, but nor can he be made to live in the home without her. He has not rejected his father nor denied the validity of divination.

A new situation created by a Society dominated by whites gives him a way out. But it is not a happy exit. He decides to 'banish himself' to the 'city of gold,' to leave behind his parents, his wives, his kin, his home. The witch wife begs to go with him but to that he cannot agree. He is escaping, but he is not emancipated.

His mother and Bigwapi, the main sufferers, ask a fundamental question. 'Where does the power of witchcraft lie when you know that you have performed no deliberate destructive act?' The answer given by Bigwapi herself, in a flash of self-realisation, is 'I am a witch, in my heart.' And, left alone on the stage, NaboSikova, representing all the multifaceted roles of mother, mother-in-law, wife, daughter, daughter-in-law, affirms: 'That is the case with every woman.'

Los Angeles,   Hilda Kuper
April, 1969

CHARACTERS IN ORDER OF APPEARANCE[1]

NTAMO ZWANE	:	Old Father of Sikova
NABOSIKOVA	:	Mother of Sikova
INDUNA	:	Councillor of Ntamo
BIGWAPI	:	Second Wife of Sikova
LOMUSA	:	Young Sister of Bigwapi
JOBENI	:	Friend of Sikova
SIKOVA	:	Only living Child of Ntamo. About 36 years old.
LAHLOPE Senior	:	First Wife of Sikova
LAHLOPE Junior	:	Third Wife of Sikova, and Sister of LaHlope Senior
HELEMU } MZULULEKE }	:	Brothers of Ntamo
FERDINAND	:	A Townsman
PETER	:	Postman
ELIAS	:	A Townsman
TEKANI	:	Child of LaHlope Senior
MANCHUMAN	:	Witch Doctor
MARTHA	:	Shebeen Queen
POLICEMAN & CHORUS		

The play takes place over a period of a year

ACT I	Scene 1	Swazi Homestead
	Scene 2	Outside Swazi Homestead
	Scene 3	Same as Scene 1
	Scene 4	Same as Scene 2
ACT II	Scene 1	Outside Factory
	Scene 2	Same as Act I, Scene 1
	Scene 3	Same as Scene 1
ACT III	Scene 1	Room in Johannesburg Township
	Scene 2	Swaziland — symbolic representation
	Scene 3	Same as Act I, Scene 1
ACT IV	Scene 1	Shebeen
	Scene 2	Same as Act I, Scene 1

Produced and published in Zulu translation.

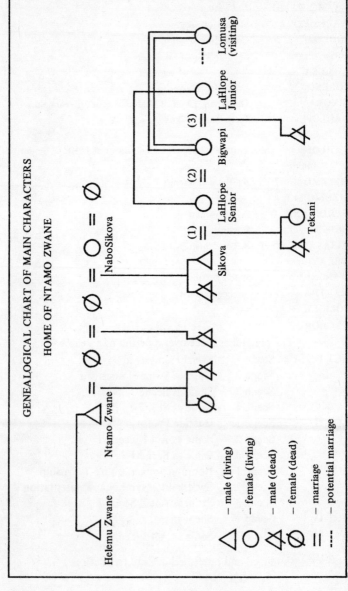

GENEALOGICAL CHART OF MAIN CHARACTERS
HOME OF NTAMO ZWANE

△ — male (living)
○ — female (living)
⬘ — male (dead)
⬖ — female (dead)
= — marriage
⋯ — potential marriage

Helemu Zwane
Ntamo Zwane
NaboSikova
Sikova
LaHlope Senior (1)
Bigwapi (2)
LaHlope Junior (3)
Lomusa (visiting)
Tekani

Act 1

SCENE ONE

Music in background. The yard of a Swazi homestead with a background of circular reed fencing and a hut in the corner. Ntamo Zwane a head-ringed councillor is squatting on the ground when his wife NaboSikova comes in carrying a hoe. She walks into the hut and comes out without the hoe, and sits beside him.

NTAMO: You are home early from the field, mother of Sikova?

NABOSIKOVA: I was tired. The sun killed me.

NTAMO: It is killing us all — the whole world is withering.

NABOSIKOVA: The fields are white for want of rain.

NTAMO: What will we eat this year?

NABOSIKOVA: We will swallow the pickings of our teeth.   *Proverbs?*

NTAMO: They might fill your stomach, old woman, but they won't fill mine.

[*He laughs, and points to a space in his mouth.*]

NABOSIKOVA: A woman is used to munching the scrapings of the pot!

NTAMO: [*meaningly*] Some want more than scrapings! They want the meat as well! Where are the daughters-in-law now?

NABOSIKOVA: The big LaHlope went to gather wood and her little co-wife went with her.[2]

NTAMO: The little wife went as well! You must be careful, mother of Sikova. There are too few children in our home. Too many stones lie on the ground. Sikova is our only living fruit, and his seed must be guarded well. The little wife might be carrying the son that will make us all rejoice. She should not seek danger. Why didn't the second wife go in her stead?

NABOSIKOVA: Bigwapi! She refused, my lord.

NTAMO: For what reason?

NABOSIKOVA: What shall I say? — 'My foot is sore,' 'my head is sore.' Always some excuse to stay behind alone!

NTAMO: Listen, mother of Sikova. I have seen things I do not like, and heard evil whispers in the grass.

NABOSIKOVA: Sometimes people whisper on purpose to make trouble.

NTAMO: Silence woman! I am old, and know what I am saying. We Swazi have too much jealousy! Sometimes the son covets the father's stool before it is empty, and greedy brothers fight to grab the cattle of the home; and youths want women that their kinsmen still enjoy. But there is no jealousy like that between the wives of the same man. Then every gentle feeling can be thrust aside, and spite and fear and hate can rule and act! It is then that witchcraft enters and homes are turned to graves!

NABOSIKOVA: You have spoken, and I will not hide from you that my heart too is heavy.

NTAMO: What have you seen?

NABOSIKOVA: Perhaps nothing — perhaps everything! A little speck of dust can become an ant-heap in a mother's eyes, but I noticed today that though Bigwapi said her foot was sore she did not limp when weeding in the fields.

NTAMO: Was she alone?

NABOSIKOVA: Yes — she went before me but we came back together.

NTAMO: Why does she avoid the others? Does she not know that wives must work together? Their joint hands must produce the food that puts their husband's name in many mouths. Can she not see that it is wrong always to work alone, always to be different, always to be the cold person at the hearth? What power has she thus to remain aloof?

 NABOSIKOVA: Her power is in her heart, Zwane. It is full of sorrow.

NTAMO: Sorrow!?

NABOSIKOVA: Yes, Zwane. Sorrow that increases to see the little
wife in her fruitfulness.

NTAMO: Whom does she blame that she herself is barren as a
stone? She should be grateful that we keep her here at all
and don't return her whence she came and use the cattle we
gave for her to marry one who would fill our huts with life.[3]

NABOSIKOVA: That is heavy, oh Zwane, heavy indeed. I pity her.

NTAMO: I have paid too much for pity. My cattle kraal is empty
paying medicine-men brought by our son to cure her.

NABOSIKOVA: He loves her greatly.

NTAMO: Love! What thing is that with which to kill our home!
Our home is empty that should be filled with the lowing of
cattle, the beating of corn between the grindstones, and the
singing and crying of children. Indeed the cattle have gone,
and the women are silent for we do not see the children. Is
this love? A home is built by respect, and strength, and
truth in self. These are the things desired by the ancestors.
These are their rules. Then they will help with health, and
corn, and children. But where the ancient laws are thrown
aside and a man thinks only of his desires, the home is weak,
and witches strike to kill. My forefathers were councillors of
Kings, and my sons and his sons must wake again their
empty huts.[4] I do not want our line to end. Sikova is your
son, and you must stop this trouble.

NABOSIKOVA: Do not blame me, my husband. As you say – he
is my son, my only living son. His life is mine, and well I
know that I, his mother, must try to keep the peace between
his wives. But it is not easy when a man has three wives,
and one is Bigwapi! I try to see he does not choose between
them; that if he gives to one he gives to all; that if he buys a
blanket he buys three; that if a pot is needed it shall be
shared; that when he cuts his land he does not keep the
fertile part separate, and leave the others scratching stones.
But his desires I cannot divide for him – his heart pushes

him where I cannot guide.

NTAMO: There he is foolish — jealousy grows where too much love is shown, for women do not reason. This you should know.

NABOSIKOVA: I also know that there are things men choose to forget. I have often warned our son, but still he spends more nights with her whose womb was never filled. He always hopes for her, and in his pity shows his love.

NTAMO: To have many women is the nature of man. You women need children to fulfil yourselves.

NABOSIKOVA: Yes, Zwane. Without them life is lonely by day and night

[*Sounds of praises coming from outside*]

Ntamo son of Tekwane of Puhlapi

You of the Mountain

You who roll over the small stones

Background Music. [*Enter: An Induna followed by Bigwapi, Lomusa, and two other girls. Lomusa and the two girls are carrying beer. They place one bowl in front of NaboSikova. Bigwapi leads them into the store hut where they leave the others. They come out and sit down near NaboSikova. The Induna has squatted within the gateway.*]

INDUNA: *Nkosi!*[5] This beer was sent from Bigwapi's home to you, her father and her mother.

CHORUS: *Nkosi!*

NTAMO: Greetings my children.

GIRLS: Greetings.

NABOSIKOVA: When did you come? We did not see you arrive?

BIGWAPI: They brought it while we were in the fields.

NABOSIKOVA: [*smiling*] It must have been our ancestors that made us hurry home.

NTAMO: [*with dignity*] Your family has helped us this day, my children. We were very dry. Let us taste its sweetness.

NABOSIKOVA: [*to Bigwapi*] Fetch a strainer.

[*Bigwapi enters the hut at the back, and returns with strainer and small bowl.*]

NABOSIKOVA: How are the folk at home?

LOMUSA: They are still well.

NABOSIKOVA: When did you leave home?

LOMUSA: At sunrise. We did not rest till we arrived. It is a long
way to walk now that the white folk have closed their farms
in barbed-wire fences, and we have to find a way round like
hares in a hunt.

INDUNA: [*indignantly*] They have no right to tie their land with
barbed-wire and keep us out like animals. They are just
thieves — they steal everything!

NTAMO: [*a little indulgently*] It does not help you, *Nduna,*[6] to
kick your feet against barbed-wire!

[*Bigwapi strains a little of the beer off the top, then, kneel-
ing, drinks a little and hands the bowl to her father-in-law.*]

NTAMO: [*to the girls*] What are you eating at your place?

LOMUSA: We eat nothing. We have to buy from the shop this
year, or starve.

NTAMO: We also eat nothing here.

NABOSIKOVA: [*who has been watching the girl*] You have grown
big, Lomusa.

BIGWAPI: Oh, she is still small.

[*Lomusa looks down in embarrassment and says nothing.*]

NTAMO: It is a pity you find us hungry, child of my age-mate.

[*turns to the Induna*] Go, and look for a chicken to welcome
them.[7]

CHORUS: *Nkosi!* Zwane!

[*Lomusa and the Girls take this as their dismissal and move
off after the Induna.*]

NTAMO: [*thoughtfully*] That girl might help us in our troubles.
As you know, according to our law I need only give one
extra beast to keep her as our son's wife, and seed-bearer to
her sister. I would rather give that beast for her than waste
it on more doctors. Since the elder is a dried-out pool let us
fill it before we die of thirst. It might help her too.

NABOSIKOVA: I don't think it will help Bigwapi. A child may
   be taught to call another woman 'mother,' but its mouth
   remembers from whose breasts it drank its milk.

NTAMO: You know everything! But I think the girl was sent here
   for a purpose. The cattle that I gave her father for his
   daughter have already gone to fetch a wife for his son. If I
   demand them back he is tied up in a knot, and I think fore-
   seeing this, he sent the girl to fill the empty carrying sling
   on Bigwapi's back.[8] You must speak to Sikova.

NABOSIKOVA: As you say, so I will do.
   [*Enter Sikova*]

SIKOVA: [*respectfully*] Father, I was looking for you. Jobeni
   brought a message that we are called for a meeting at the
   District Office tomorrow.

NTAMO: Another meeting! They think we have nothing better to
   do than say, '*Nkosi*,' '*Nkosi*.'[9]
   [*Sikova looks at the bowl.*]
   Drink.
   [*Sikova kneels and drinks.*]

SIKOVA: *Nkosi*, father. Where did this sweet beer come from?

NABOSIKOVA. From Bigwapi's home.

SIKOVA: [*smiling with pleasure*] *Hau, bantu.*[10] Who brought it?

NTAMO: Your sister-in-law. Bigwapi's little sister.

SIKOVA: Lomusa! It is a long time since I saw her.

NTAMO: She has grown up now.

NABOSIKOVA: Yes indeed! She is ready for marriage.

NTAMO: I gave ten cattle for her sister.

NABOSIKOVA: Perhaps it would please the elder to have the
   younger with her always.

NTAMO: That's right.

SIKOVA: [*laughing*] Three wives are enough for me, father. They
   eat too much, and talk too much.

NTAMO: [*seriously*] You have not got three wives! A woman
   without a child is no wife. It is not for such that we fathers
   give our cattle.

SIKOVA: You have always helped me, father. But this would be
no help. Where will I find for her the food to eat? Where
will I cut for her the garden that she needs? My wives are
crying that they are hungry, that they have no land.
Yesterday the big LaHlope grumbled that her fields were
over-worked, and she and Bigwapi began to hit each other
with words.

NTAMO: Do not criticise your big wife, my son. She is a woman
who is right. She is quiet and full of respect, and like your
mother, she does not start quarrels.

SIKOVA: Excuse me, father, but does not Bigwapi show respect?

NTAMO: I did not say otherwise. Before me she is always humble,
but there is no person who can see into the heart of another.
But all this talk of women turns my head. Call Jobeni.
[*Exit Sikova.*]

NABOSIKOVA: I must look in my store hut for food for the girls.

NTAMO: [*takes drink from the bowl and hands it to NaboSikova
saying, magnanimously*] Drink, Mother.[11] You may finish
the pot.

NABOSIKOVA: *Nkosi*, Zwane. You of the Mountains.
[*NaboSikova enters the hut as Sikova, Jobeni and the
Induna come through the doorway. They sit down.*]

NTAMO: Well, Jobeni, what is this you come to tell me?

JOBENI: I was sent by the new little office chief — the one we
named 'White-eyes' — to call you to the Court House.

NTAMO: What for is this meeting?

JOBENI: The messenger did not know. He only said White-eyes
wanted us on time.

INDUNA: On time! Let him come by *his* feet on time! He will
fly across the roads in his motor car, throwing so much dust
over us that he won't even see us, and when we come in
after him he will look at his watch and say, 'You Swazi are
always late,' and stamp his foot.

NTAMO: Yes — how foolish these Whites are. Three years ago
they said I was too old to pay my tax but each year since I

must appear to show I still have no teeth! Do you think this
meeting is to do with tax?

JOBENI: I'm afraid so.

NTAMO: Well, we'll see.

INDUNA: Will you then leave the killing of the girls' chicken for
after the meeting?

NTAMO: No, of course not. The office can wait for us. I promised
the girls first. Come, Induna, show me which one you chose.
[*The two old men go off.*]

SIKOVA: Jobeni, I am in trouble.

JOBENI: What is it, my age-mate?

SIKOVA: Did you see some girls with Bigwapi?

JOBENI: Indeed I did! While you were with your father I was not
wasting my time.

SIKOVA: Well, one of them is my *mlamu*[12] and my parents want
me to take her to bear for Bigwapi.

JOBENI: Oh you are a lucky fellow! What did she say?

SIKOVA: Who? Bigwapi?

JOBENI: No, your *mlamu*.

SIKOVA: I haven't even seen her.

JOBENI: Well, I have. She looks like Bigwapi, and having seen her
it is hard to turn away the eyes.

SIKOVA: That must be her, but I don't want her.

JOBENI: Why? What are you saying? Is there a man who does not
want two queens, each beautiful as the shining sun?

SIKOVA: There is only one sun, and I want no more wives.

JOBENI: Well, your father cannot force you, and I am willing to
help.

SIKOVA: You? How?

JOBENI: I'll try for myself — I have been a bachelor long enough.
When next I go to the mines I'll turn gold into cows for that
girl.

SIKOVA: You are speaking the truth. Oh my friend, we will be
real brothers. Until you spoke I could not see the light. There
are things happening in my home that make me feel afraid.

Sometimes when I call my wives to speak with me, I find
silence where there should be laughter. And sometimes
when I am offered beer by one there is bitterness on the
tongues of the others. There have been men who fled
their homes for less, but I am no wanderer. A man should
only leave his home because he must keep it whole.

END OF SCENE 1

SCENE TWO

*The two wives – the Big LaHlope and the Little LaHlope are
returning from their wood-gathering, each with a bundle on her
head. The Big LaHlope is in front.*

LAHLOPE Snr: Stop, sister! Look, there are some people in
    Bigwapi's yard. I cannot see who they are – can you?

LAHLOPE Jnr: No. I can only see that they are girls in *mahiya*.[13]

LAHLOPE Snr: That's mother talking to them.

LAHLOPE Jnr: Let's rest awhile, and watch. This wood is heavy.

LAHLOPE Snr: You are carrying more than wood.

LAHLOPE Jnr: Indeed I am. It must be a boy. It already kicks so
    much. Do you think it is a boy?

LAHLOPE Snr: Yes, it is all in the back, but you cannot be sure.
    It is still small, and you must just wait.

LAHLOPE Jnr: I wish I had not so long a time to wait. Sometimes
    I feel afraid.

LAHLOPE Snr: All women do. To have a child is pain.

LAHLOPE Jnr: It is not pain I fear. It is something worse.

LAHLOPE Snr: Don't speak of it.

LAHLOPE Jnr: I will – to you. It doesn't help that each time I
    want to speak of it you say I must be quiet. I have kept
    silent too long, but no one can sew up my mouth.

LAHLOPE Snr: Speak then. But when we are not under four eyes[14]

I will not listen or you will get us all in trouble.

LAHLOPE Jnr: All right, I will try. I am afraid of her! Did you
notice her garden when we passed by? Part of it was
freshly weeded. She must have gone there again this morning,
but when you wanted her to come with you she cried, 'my
body aches all over.'

LAHLOPE Snr: Perhaps the aches get better when we go.

LAHLOPE Jnr: Sister, do not let us deceive ourselves. She hates
us. Is it not strange that there is only one garden bearing
good food this year?

LAHLOPE Snr: Do not wake that again. On that account I nearly
quarrelled with our husband.

LAHLOPE Jnr: But it is true. In all the other fields the heads of
corn are small as a child's fist, and the stalks are brittle as
fire sticks. But in hers the heads are full and the plants
stand as high as this [*gestures*] . Has she not medicine to
steal our food away and take it for herself? And I will tell
you something else! Yesterday mother sent me to her hut
to fetch a spoon, and I saw a pot in the corner. I peeped
inside to see if there was something nice to eat, and in it
was a big root that looked like *gebeleweni* which grows on
precipices and is always green. I have been told that it is
used to steal the hearts of men and make them weak so that
they are overcome with desire when she appears who called
their name in plucking it!

LAHLOPE Snr: Sister, I tremble. You know our father-in-law did
not really want our husband to marry her. She was promised
to another, and was about to go to him when she saw our
husband at the King's festival. She stole him then with her
love potions.

LAHLOPE Jnr: Do you think the man she should have married
threw on her the sickness that she suffers now?

LAHLOPE Snr: I do not know. When first she came into this home
I helped her, and when the years went by and still she had
no child I pitied her, but never will I forget the day my own

child lay ill and that one found me weeping and said, 'Why do you weep? You can bear others.'

LAHLOPE Jnr: Evil is her tongue, and dark her heart!

LAHLOPE Snr: Yes, we must be careful. Look, mother has left and she sits alone with one of the girls.

LAHLOPE Jnr: I wonder what they are whispering about.

[BLACK-OUT to Scene One]

BIGWAPI: Lomusa, tell me things of home. You don't know how I long for you all. All the days I remember my friends, and the great freedom of girlhood; and the spring where we bathed, and the time I went to our mother's sister at the King's capital where I first saw my husband.

LOMUSA: We think of you also, sister. When will you visit us?

BIGWAPI: I do not know — there is no chicken that scratches for another. During my last visit home cattle strayed into my garden, and rain seeped into my new grain-pit so that half my millet was rotted, and my co-wives looked on and did nothing!

LOMUSA: What sort of co-wives are those?

BIGWAPI: Never can I tell you. At first the Big One welcomed me since I took over her duties as hand-maiden to the mother, but when she saw our husband's eyes on me her heart disappeared in thoughts for herself; and from the beginning her little sister-wife has looked upon herself as a Queen — a Queen of the bees to whom we should all bring honey.

LOMUSA: Is she lazy?

BIGWAPI: Yes, she is lazy, and the truth is that we do not feel for each other.

LOMUSA: At home they think you are well treated here. Why don't you tell them how it is?

BIGWAPI: They can do nothing. When I got married I rejoiced. Even in the cattle-kraal singing the songs of farewell to my home I had to force the tears. Now I hear those sad songs in my heart all the time.

[*Softly she sings – Mekeza song.*]
    'Now I remember mother
    Oh come rescue me, my brothers. . .'
[*She begins to weep.*]

LOMUSA: No, sister, don't.

BIGWAPI: In front of *you* I don't mind if I weep. In front of *them* I must pretend my heart is like a grind-stone which, when they strike, becomes only sharper.

LOMUSA: And your husband?

BIGWAPI: It is because of him that they are eaten with envy. They see that he treats me well and finds it sweet for us to be together. All that he can he does for me, but I am alone. As you know, I like work; I like the earth and the things that grow in it. When I plant I feel the seed creating for me. All the work of women is my delight. I do not read a book, but from the earth I learn of many things. Had I a child I could teach him much.

LOMUSA: What do the medicine men say?

BIGWAPI: One says this, and one says that, so that the truth is hidden, as the blind mole running under the ground.
[*Both women look up, startled, as Sikova enters and squats. For a moment there is silence. The women turn their faces away, and look down.*]

SIKOVA: Greetings, my *mlamu*.

LOMUSA: Greetings to you.
[*Between Lomusa and Sikova there is a relationship of familiarity which is completely different from the respect and shyness which she must exhibit in front of his parents.*]

BIGWAPI: Lay down the mat, Lomusa.
[*Lomusa unrolls mat for Sikova.*]

SIKOVA: Did you come well?

LOMUSA: Yes, though it would have been easier if I had been a horse and could have jumped the fences. The paths have burnt our feet.

SIKOVA: Where are the others who came with you?

LOMUSA: They are so tired that they are sleeping. I will wake them when the food is cooked.

SIKOVA: That was good beer in the great hut.

LOMUSA: [*laughing*] Of course! It was brought by me!

BIGWAPI: Yes, we put a big pot aside for you.

SIKOVA: Go and get it, *mlamu*. My throat is still so dry it whistles when I talk to you.

LOMUSA: I am dry as well. [*She goes into the hut.*]

SIKOVA: [*looking after her*] Time passes fast. There is a miracle in growing up and seeing the seed appear in each flower. She is a maiden now.

BIGWAPI: Your father also thought so!

SIKOVA: I want to speak to you about it.

[*Lomusa returns with the beer. She kneels in front of Sikova, sips, and hands it to him.*]

I left Jobeni in the barracks — fetch him to drink with us.

LOMUSA: Me! How will I see him?

SIKOVA: [*laughing*] Don't trouble yourself — he will see you all right!

BIGWAPI: Well, she has gone. What is your secret?

SIKOVA: Do you not know it.

BIGWAPI: I am a woman, and keep my secrets hidden — even from myself.

SIKOVA: [*slightly ill at ease*] Why did your father send this girl?

BIGWAPI: To bring some beer.

SIKOVA: Is there nothing more for the mouth than beer?

BIGWAPI: What else do you want?

SIKOVA: Nothing.

BIGWAPI: Tell me.

SIKOVA: She is your sister — borne by one mother.

BIGWAPI: So that's it. You agree with your parents.

SIKOVA: I did not say I did. It is for you to speak. Would you be happy to have her with you? To have her child as yours?

BIGWAPI: That would not help me. The others would not love me more on its account — [*hesitating*] and you?

SIKOVA: Yes?

BIGWAPI: You might love me less?

SIKOVA: No, that is not so. I am a ripe man now and know myself. For me you will have no equal. It will always be as when I found you at the King's dance. Though I knew you were betrothed to another, I could not stop. My first wife, chosen for me by my father, wiped away the darkness of my youth. I respect her like a mother and do not criticise her, but you and I are one. I have no need for others to rejoice my body. If I take girls it is not for joy, but to increase the home. That is why, should the Little LaHlope have a son, we can all be thankful.

BIGWAPI: Yes, we can all be thankful. You will have a son to lengthen your shadow, your own son to suceed you.

SIKOVA: To succeed me! Never before have I heard you speak evil. Is not a successor chosen only when the father himself is dead? I am not so old that I should look upon a son and say, 'He will take my place when I no longer am,' but in my lifetime, in my health, I want him. He is my body, he is with my being. Through me my ancestors made a Queen with child.

BIGWAPI: I did not want to anger you. It is for you I want a son.

SIKOVA: I will try with all my strength that you will bear me a son. I will seek stronger medicine.

BIGWAPI: Already my sickness has eaten the cattle of the fathers. Medicine men demand money.

SIKOVA: I will look for it, and I will find it.

BIGWAPI: Where is money? We are poor. We eat what we plant, and still our navels disappear within. We have no money. We have nothing to sell.

SIKOVA: No, we have ourselves to sell. My own words force me — a man should only leave his home to keep it whole. On your account I will go out to work — not here. Here there is no money. I will go to the place of Gold — the place of wonders — Goli.[15] I have not been there before, and, until now, I have never wanted to go.

BIGWAPI: Oh my husband, do not go so far. It will be too
    lonely without you. Do not go.

SIKOVA: Woman! What do you want? First you drive me to
    look for money and when I promise to find it you hold me
    back. I feel like a buck in a bushfire.

BIGWAPI: I did not want to chase you away. Stay. Take my
    sister to bear for me. I do not want to be without you. I do
    not want you to lose yourself in the city of gold. You are
    my —

SIKOVA: Quiet woman! They come.
    [*Jobeni and Lomusa return Jobeni sits at a respectful
    distance from Bigwapi, who continues grinding without
    looking up.*]

LOMUSA: I found him!

SIKOVA: Did you have to look for him over all the mountains
    and in the caves?

JOBENI: Do you mean I come slowly when called for a drink!
    What has happened to me?
    [*Enter the two Hlope Wives.*]

LAHLOPE Snr: We too have come to greet your sister. We heard
    she was visiting you.

END OF SCENE TWO

SCENE THREE

*Same as Scene One. Ntamo, his Induna, Helemu, Mzululeke and
Sikova are squatting on the ground.*

NTAMO: Next time when White-eyes calls us to a meeting I will
    say that I don't hear in my ears and don't see with my
    eyes, and to go to the meeting would just waste my senses!

INDUNA: I will pretend that I am dumb, and since I cannot speak

I had better stay behind with the women!

NTAMO: Really Whites talk nonsense. They will destroy us.
Never will I agree to sell my cattle. They are our life — we
eat them; we milk them; we plough with them; we pray
with them. We Blacks do not know how to live without
them.

INDUNA: How can we sell our cattle unless they give us something else to look after us?

NTAMO: What can they give instead of cattle?

INDUNA: They could give us money.

NTAMO: Money! That thing! It does not multiply. It does not
grow! Even if the Government gave me enough money to
feed me and my children until I die, I still would not want
to stay without my cattle. It is nonsense to say that cattle
are money.

SIKOVA: Let me not stab your tongue, father.[16] I agree with all
you said, but things go by money nowadays and not by
cattle. Today we eat money; we buy with money; we dress
with money.

NTAMO: Leave off! Would you be happy to throw away the ways
of the Ancients and follow the road of the Whites? Would
you buy a wife with money?

SIKOVA: No, my father, I would not buy a wife with money.
Yet I cannot care for the wives I have, without money. For
everything they want I must pay money, and it is not the
penny that helps. You heard White-eyes say that soon it
would be time for tax again, and for each wife I must pay
10/- cash and 35/- for my own head.[17] If I have not the
money I will be kicked into gaol.

INDUNA: [*gloomily*] What do they do with all the money that
we give them?

NTAMO: They say they build schools and roads, but you can
never belive them.

INDUNA: [*gloomily*] It is so. The world is upside down.

NTAMO: [*to Sikova*] Last year when I had to pay your tax I sold

an ox. Not a little one – not a calf; an ox indeed. A
three-year old, with horns curved as a Koodoo buck and
skin so smooth that the King himself would welcome it for
his dancing shield, and Shorty, the trader, gave me L5 cash
and one bag of corn! [*working himself up*] No! I will not
sell an ox again. I will ask for L200 for one head, and if the
White man argues I will not listen. I will no longer sell my
cattle. They can sell me first!

SIKOVA: Father, I will sell myself. Money is needed at our home. I
will look for work.

NTAMO: Tax time is not yet here – you can wait awhile.

SIKOVA: No, father, I have been thinking over the matter. Better
go now and be back for ploughing time next year.

NTAMO: [*startled*] Ploughing time? Next year? Where are you
going?

SIKOVA: To the place where money is – to Goli.

NTAMO: Where?

SIKOVA: I said Goli.

NTAMO: But you do not know Goli. You have never moved from
Swaziland. Why so far? Why not work as before on a farm
nearby, and come back when we want you?

SIKOVA: The treatment is bad on farms, father. I am no longer a
child to be shouted at every day, and I am not an ox to be
driven by a whip; and even when they look on me as a man
they only pay 10/- a month.

NTAMO: My heart does not wish you to go but I cannot stand in
front of you. What work will you do?

SIKOVA: I do not know. Perhaps I will join the mines.

NTAMO: Never! I agree that you can go away to work in the
town, but I will never agree that you go down the hole! Do
you want to die, as your own brother, born of your own
mother, died? Who will then look after your wives? You
shall not go to the mines!

SIKOVA: All right, father, I listen. I thought of the mines because
Jobeni will be returning there in a short time and he could

help me. I do not know the work of the towns. My work is
with earth, and animals. But I suppose something will turn
up. After all, boys with no sense come back with money
and goods, and stories of things that make me gape.

NTAMO: They are just lying; the only thing they pick up is the
sickness of the woman.

SIKOVA: Do not fear for me, father. I only go to build up my
home. In my absence my little wife will bear my child, and
I will return with money for food, and clothes, and tax, and
even medicine men.

NTAMO: I see you are speaking the truth, my son. You are not
running away.

SIKOVA: No, father, it is only for money that I go. I am grown
now, and there are many things I see we need.

NTAMO: You are grown only by the White man's laws. As long as
I am living you are beneath my hands.[18]

SIKOVA: Father, I know I am not free.

NTAMO: I will say no more. Have you spoken to your mother?

SIKOVA: No.

NTAMO: Induna, call her now, she's in her cooking hut. [*to Sikova*]
You must take care of the money that you earn in the town
and not waste it. Also, I believe that the Place of Gold is
full of robbers, so you must hide it as soon as you are paid,
then send it straight home. Do not keep much or you will
throw it away on nothings. I will buy a few bags of corn when
we need them, and the rest I will use to buy cattle. That is
our best bank. And when you come back you will see about
the girl.

SIKOVA: I beg you not to take her for me while I am away. Use
the money for food and cattle, but nothing else. It is not
for her that I am going from here, but to keep what I have.

NTAMO: You are obstinate, but I will not force you, and we will
wait till you return.
[*Enter Induna with NaboSikova*]
Sit, mother of Sikova. Something has happened and it is no

use running round it as though we were hunting a lion in
the forest. This boy wants to go to work in Johannesburg.
I do not like it, but I have agreed. He thinks he is a man and
stands in the White man's law. What do you, his mother,
say?

NABOSIKOVA: [*speaking slowly*] Johannesburg! Sikova! It is
something that I have often feared to hear — a thing I have
pressed down. [*passionately*] From what are you running
away? What has destroyed you in your home? Is it not
enough that one son lies beneath the stones of gold?

SIKOVA: I will not work in the mines, mother.

NABOSIKOVA: I do not want him to go to the city. Why do they
go — the young and the strong?

NTAMO: Do not be so foolish and ask 'why do they go?' Does
money come from you for tax? And you, you women, drive
them forth as well by shouting 'Go, be a man and fight for
gold and bring us clothes, and beads, and shiny things, and
tell us wonders that lie beyond our fields.' You women send
them forth and then you weep because they want to go!

NABOSIKOVA: No, my lord. No, Zwane. No, it is not so. No
mother ever sent her son to fight in the White man's world.
Young foolish girls may desire that, but not those like me —
not mothers.

SIKOVA: Mother, it is necessary. I am old now and must look
after myself.

NABOSIKOVA: To me you are still small. As long as your father
lives you are still small and in his armpit.

NTAMO: Remember that, my son. Do not go the ways of the
White people whose children make themselves bigger than
their parents. We know the right laws. Mother of Sikova,
fetch the wives.

[*Exit NaboSikova.*]

HELEMU: What do my brothers say? We have heard but give us
again your reasons for leaving the home, son.

MZULULEKE: Yes, child of our place, tell us again.

SIKOVA: It is not a long story, my fathers. I am a man now and
see that this year I will have no food with which to feed my
people, and no money to pay tax.

HELEMU: With whom will you go?

SIKOVA: I will go alone.

HELEMU: Have you spoken to your wives?

SIKOVA: [*slight hesitation*] No, they will see my reason and will
remain well at home. You, my fathers, will care for them
and see that they do not go outside the law. They are not
women who hit birds for a man in his absence.[19]

HELEMU: Do they stay well together?

NTAMO: They stay like women. And where there are women
there are always words, and where there are women's words
there is always jealousy.

HELEMU: [*wisely*] Sometimes jealousy is woken by the man
and it is less when the man has gone away.

NTAMO: You are right, my brother. And his mother will watch
over them. They listen to her.

HELEMU: Let the teacher write for you the address of your
cousin in Johannesburg. He left many years ago, but we
still have his address, and he must have learned a lot by now.

NTAMO: [*impatiently*] How can a man who does not return
home teach my son a lot? It would be better if he were not
taught by such a one!

HELEMU: Even if he did not teach him he could still stay with
him till he finds work. It is always better to go to people of
your own blood than to wander among strangers.

NTAMO: All right. We will get his address.

[*Enter Wives with Mother. They sit.*]

NTAMO: We have called you Queens to tell you that your husband
is leaving soon for the city. He is not running away from you,
but is going to work for you. While he is away you must stay
quietly and in peace.

HELEMU: We, his fathers, will watch his affairs at home.

SIKOVA: [*gratefully*] Father! Zwane!

NTAMO: We will wait for him at home, and he will send back
        money while he is away to buy grain to feed the family.
        And if we need no more grain, I will buy cattle for him.

SIKOVA: Yes, it is money that I must go. That which binds
        me to my home will wait for my return.

NABOSIKOVA: [*realizing that there is no more that she can do, asks
        sadly*] When will you go, my son?

SIKOVA: I could go as soon as I have fixed my papers with
        White-eyes. It is best to go quickly. Farewells are pain.
        [*trying to put a brave face on the whole thing.*]
        When I leave home my baggage will be light. A little bundle
        of food for the road, and a few clothes tied in a blanket,
        but, when I return I will have a big heavy box bursting with
        gifts!

NTAMO: Quiet! Do not open your mouth too wide.

END OF SCENE THREE

SCENE FOUR

*Jobeni is lounging around when Lomusa appears, and on seeing
her he pounces out, shouting:*

JOBENI: Pretty girls fall in and out of love. There's never a heart
        that remains empty. Even your heart won't be empty for
        long. Come here, girl. It is you I am talking to. [*He makes a
        grab at her.*] *Hau!* What lovely breasts, and eyelashes long
        as those of the doe. Turn around and let me look at you
        properly.

LOMUSA: [*pretending indignation*] *Ai suka!* Be off!

JOBENI: Those legs. Those thighs. My heart beats like the engine
        of the tin mine. If only those legs could walk in the yard of
        my home. When will you woo me?

LOMUSA: [*laughing defiantly*] Never!

JOBENI: Am I so ugly?

LOMUSA: Of course you are ugly, and wicked too!

JOBENI: Then mix my ugliness with your beauty, and my
wickedness with your sweetness.

LOMUSA: You are crazy.

JOBENI: Of course I am crazy. Since I saw you I have been crazy.
I shake when my eyes look at you — don't you see I need a
blanket?

LOMUSA: [*laughing*] Don't touch me.

JOBENI: I have been thinking of you for two days and two nights.
Even a poor man with no cattle eats meat. I have been
thinking of you since I saw you.

LOMUSA: My, how you run!

JOBENI: Of course, I am no tortoise! But listen girl. I am not
laughing now; don't you go to anyone else but me.

LOMUSA: Hau! Are you my husband already?

JOBENI: No, I cannot yet beat you — I can only beseech you.

LOMUSA: With what do you beseech me? Words cannot be seen.

JOBENI: Wait and see. [*laughing*] I have ten head of cattle hidden
for you in the mine.
[*Enter Sikova*]

SIKOVA: We have finished the business, my friend, and they have
agreed. [*to Lomusa*] Go to your sister, she needs you. [*He
sits, wearily.*]

SIKOVA: What a bad day. How are things with you?

JOBENI: I think she likes me. She swears at me nicely!

SIKOVA: Good. Remember, I am leaving her for you. I will tell
Bigwapi to keep her here for company until I return, so that
when you are gone as well no one else can grab her. I wish
that you were coming with me, Jobeni, but they would not
hear of my going to the mine.

JOBENI: They are foolish about it. Witches strike no matter
where you are. They don't need rocks to kill, nor holes!
Why don't you tell them?

SIKOVA: [*with dignity*] I do not like to argue with my elders.

JOBENI: Even so, we should have gone together, brother. I would have taught you. Town is not easy and [*a trifle shamefaced*] all the stories I have told you about it have not been true. You might find it hard to get work.

SIKOVA: [*impatiently*] I am no child. When we meet there it is I who will tell you things.

JOBENI: I will rejoice with you. What do your Queens say?

SIKOVA: They said nothing, but I did not like the way they looked at *her* as if they knew she was the cause; while she looked down as though she did not hear, or care. And yet I must go. Though the path twists and I know not where it leads, still I must go.

END OF SCENE FOUR

Act 2

Outside a factory. A group of Africans squatting on the pavement in the lunch-hour, playing a game with stones. A main road nearby. Noise of traffic every now and then drowns the comments of the players. The men are in rather ragged clothing. A man on a bicycle rides across, backstage, singing. 'I will always love you.' A player shouts back, 'What bachelor sings that?' Players laugh and return to the game.

The main characters in the scene are: Ferdinand, a middle-aged man. Peter, in postman's uniform. Elias, who is very much the man-about-town, and a couple of other players.

FIRST PLAYER: I've hit it! [*laughter*]

SECOND PLAYER: Yes, you overcame him. Now I begin. I put mine here. [*noise of stones being moved on the pavement*]

FERDINAND: [*who is looking on*] There is a space — go on — put it there.

PETER: I bet a bob that mine wins.[20]

ELIAS: [*jeeringly*] I bet your bob has a face on both sides. Turn it round and let's see. Good, I take on your bet.
[*While the game is being played Sikova, looking very down-at-heel, moves into the background, and as he does so Elias says*]
Hau, you are slow! If I had been playing I should have kicked you out of all the holes.

SECOND PLAYER: I jump over you. [*moves his stone*]

PETER: Oh, I must hurry. I must finish him off quickly. I have a lot of letters to throw into the boxes.

24

ELIAS: Stay awhile. Don't worry too much. Why not put all the
letters in one box and come back and finish the game?

FERDINAND: No wonder, Elias, you never keep a job.

ELIAS: I would keep a job of stealing, all right! Just give me the
chance.

FERDINAND: Oh, you are a city slicker!

[*Their conversation takes place against the background of
the continuation of the game, the players saying such
things as:*

'Here is mine', 'take it', 'put him in his place', 'snap it up',
'close it', 'take if off', 'hit it'.]

[*Sound of clock striking in the distance*]

PETER: [*hurriedly*] Dammit, I must pack up. Post-office time is
the right time. [*in a very affected voice*] Punctuality is our
pass word. *Tot siens*, boys![21]

[*Other players move off saying, 'We'll see you tomorrow.'
Ferdinand, Elias and Sikova remain.*]

ELIAS: [*casually*] Got a job for me, Ferdinand?

FERDINAND: For you, Elias? Never. Do you remember the last
time I got a job for you? You got so tight that you fell
asleep in the boss's chair. [*Both men roar with laughter.*]

ELIAS: [*airily*] Never mind. I have a nice little job on hand just
now.

FERDINAND: [*meaningly*] You mean Martha?

ELIAS: Of course, Martha! Even the cops call her Shebeen Queen
AI. She is so clever, that woman. She doesn't even pay them,
they pay her!

FERDINAND: You be careful, Elias. One day you'll be caught.
One day Sergeant Frikkie will be changed, and somebody will be put in his place who doesn't like your Martha!

ELIAS: [*airily*] Don't shout your mouth off. If we are put in
prison we have the cash. The gang is tough. The customers
are the trouble. Today there are too few suckers. [*seriously*]
The trouble is we have become too respectable! Instead of
having a good time the boys either send money to their

families, or marry the women in the towns and look after
their kids, or go to the Sports Club and watch the games.
Before, the boys were here just for a little while and were so
green. They were sweet and tender, and easy to suck. Rather
like that fellow there [*pointing to Sikova*] who is listening
to us but does not understand a word of what we are saying.
His ears are filled with the language of his mother, and our
way is to him just HWE! HWE! HWE! Come, let us talk to
him.

FERDINAND: Poor fellow. All right. Let us talk to him nicely.

ELIAS: [*calls Sikova*] Come my friend.

FERDINAND: We see you.[22]

SIKOVA: I see you.

ELIAS: From where do you come, fellow?

SIKOVA: I come from Swaziland.

FERDINAND: *Hau!* I too am a Swazi. From what place in the
country of Sobhuza?

SIKOVA: From Mliba, near the river.

FERDINAND: I know the area well. Who is your Chief?

SIKOVA: My Chief is Bomu, son of Ngweja.

FERDINAND: *Hau.* A friend of my father. And what is your
name, my brother?

SIKOVA: Sikova Zwane.

FERDINAND: *Hau.* Zwane! Our clan name is one. Who is your
father?

SIKOVA: My father is Ntamo, Councillor of Kings.

FERDINAND: Shake my hand, my brother. It is sweet to meet a
countryman in the City of Gold, where men are enemies,
and to hear again the language of my home. [*The men shake
hands ceremoniously.*] Let us sit, my friend, and talk of
things of my home. It is long since I was there. [*They sit in
the gutter.*] Come stay with us, Elias.

ELIAS: No thanks. I will leave you two Swazi to talk alone.
Your tongue is too difficult for me to understand, but I
promise you, Ferdinand, that if you bring him one day to

my hide-out. I'll give him things to drink that will take the
childhood from his eyes!

FERDINAND: We shall see. Go well.

[*Elias goes off whistling loudly.*]

He is a Shangaan [*pointing to Elias*] He is not one of us,
but his beer is good. Tell me, Zwane, what brings you to
the town? What work do you seek? Where do you stay, you
stranger from the countryside?

SIKOVA: I was brought here by famine, and the need for money.
You know how it is in the country. Sometimes the rivers
rise and flood their banks and sweep the strongest mealies
in their course. And sometimes the sun shines and our
Rulers have no pity and withhold the rain.²³ So it was this
year. At home we eat nothing. We rush like locusts in search
of grass. Now I am seeking work, but I do not find it. Is
there any? Where do you work?

FERDINAND: [*proudly*] I am a messenger. You see that
bicycle — it is mine. You see, my friend. I have wonderful
references. [*very carefully he takes out of his pocket some
bedraggled sheets, and reads in halting English*]: 'To whom
it may concern. Ferdinand worked for me for 5 years and
was a good, clean, honest, reliable boy.' You read?

SIKOVA: No. I wanted to go to school but I had to herd the
cattle.

FERDINAND: [*patronisingly*] Never mind. You can get jobs
without reading your own papers. You come with me. I
have a good boss, though he sleeps a lot and I do all the
work. I will tell him that I know you from our home. I will
say you are my brother. I will find you a job.

SIKOVA: *Hau* — you are helping me. I had an address to find a
kinsman, but when I got there they told me he had left, and
since I came I have just been wandering.

FERDINAND: Tell me, are you married?

SIKOVA: Yes, I have three wives.

FERDINAND: And how many children have you?

SIKOVA: [*counting on his fingers and speaking tenderly*] The Big
    LaHlope, my first wife, has one daughter, and her little
    sister-wife is with stomach. And there is a third who has not
    yet borne a child. We are still hoping. I stay in my father's
    village and he is in charge while I am away. Though we need
    money they did not want me to go so far.
FERDINAND: It is hard to come from home, but you will grow
    used to it. I will write for you a wonderful reference. I will
    not say that you can speak English!

END OF SCENE ONE

SCENE TWO

*The same as Scene One, Act One. Some weeks later. Bigwapi and
Lomusa.*

BIGWAPI: Why are you so silent, little sister? Were you not sent
    to while away my sorrow?
LOMUSA: I was not sent to you, but to your husband, so I do
    not stay well here, and I do not help you. Now that Jobeni
    is leaving for the mines what will happen to me? Let me
    return to our home, to our mother.
BIGWAPI: As you wish. It would be easier for you away from
    me. I will tell them that you wish to go until my husband
    returns, and they will agree. Remember, I will do all I
    can to help you, for we are tied with one rope and must
    pull together. We are more than sisters now. Tomorrow,
    after work, you shall leave, and stay free as long as
    possible. There will be time enough to decide your affairs
    when Sikova himself comes back.
    [*Enter NaboSikova*]
NABOSIKOVA: I am always glad when the last fields are weeded,
    but this year it seemed that the weeds were strong and the

mealies weak, and the work went slowly. Those who helped
us weed deserve their beer. When they drink they will
remember that your husband's credit bought the grain for
it.

[*Bigwapi rises as if to go.*]

BIGWAPI: Yes, his credit is helping us already.

NABOSIKOVA: [*imperiously*] Stay here! It is not right that
since your husband left you sit all the time alone in your
hut. The inside of a hut is for sleeping, but you are not one
who sleeps in the day.

BIGWAPI: Since the pole of my hut departed I do not sleep. At
night I lie awake and dream of him.

NABOSIKOVA: It is bad to dream of one who has gone away —
it will lose him strength, and you. When a man has gone to
war his wives must stay peacefully, and quiet. The city is a
place of battle. Do not weaken my son who is fighting for
us, nor stir up trouble for those of us who must wait behind.
Stay and help us serve the beer. The little wife may be
tired.

[*sound of women in the background*]

BIGWAPI: She doesn't sound tired; nothing troubles her!

[*Two Wives come in. At first they do not see NaboSikova in
the background. LaHlope Jnr. comes in with a bundle of
green leaves. She sees Bigwapi.*]

BIGWAPI: [*coldly*] Why are you laughing?

LAHLOPE Jnr: White people do not know where to look for
manhood. They hide the above in a hat, and the below in
trousers [*shrieking with mirth*] , and so can only look at the
toes or the teeth! Jobeni said —

BIGWAPI: Quiet! Don't you see Mother is here?

LAHLOPE Jnr. [*abashed*] I did not see her.

NABOSIKOVA: So you have returned, Queens. That looks good
spinach that you found in the fields.

LAHLOPE Jnr: I have been longing for spinach all these months.

BIGWAPI: [*teasing*] You are always longing for things for your stomach.

LAHLOPE Jnr: Shut up!

BIGWAPI: I won't shut up — you're drunk!

LAHLOPE Jnr: To whom do you say 'you are drunk'? It is you
who are drunk — drunk with envy!

BIGWAPI: Envy you? A nothing!

LAHLOPE Jnr: You dung of a dog! I will strike you for that.

NABOSIKOVA: [*shouts sharply*] Silent, child!

LAHLOPE Snr: [*grabs her sister, and says, rebukingly*] Sister,
have you no respect?

LAHLOPE Jnr: [*resentfully*] Yes, but she started it.

NABOSIKOVA: Quiet, I said. Be quiet! Go fetch the big beer
pot. We can't get full on words. Go!

BIGWAPI: [*virtuously*] I will get it, mother.
[*Exit Bigwapi*]

NABOSIKOVA: [*kindly, but very seriously, to LaHlope Jnr.*] My
child, you must not look for trouble.

LAHLOPE Jnr: I know, mother. Forgive me. But when she turns
her big eyes on me I feel the thing within my womb grow
still with fear, and it is fearful for me to look at her. Have
you seen how thin she has grown? Her eyes have eaten all
her face, and her skin is dark and shines no more. She no
longer dances as before, but creeps always into her hut and
looks into tomorrow. There is hate for me in her heart.

NABOSIKOVA: Do not speak like that. Don't you know that
your best protection lies in hiding what you think and feel
from enemies?

LAHLOPE Snr: That's what I keep telling her, mother, but she
has always been hot-blooded and cannot hold her tongue.
From the time that we were children together and I carried
her on my back I've tried to protect her from herself, and
now that she is my young co-wife I often fear for her. And
now there is a reason for fear. I too feel that that woman's
jealousy shouts at me — even when her mouth is shut.

NABOSIKOVA: It is hard for all of us, my daughter. How I await my son's return.

LAHLOPE Snr: How long it seems since our husband left.

NABOSIKOVA: Hurry. The weeding party is coming.

[*Groups of men and women come in singing, and sit in groups. Beer is ladled out.*

Ntamo sits with dignity on his mat with a pot to himself. NaboSikova, Bigwapi and LaHlope Snr. scoop out the beer from huge pots. LaHlope Jnr. sits on the ground near them. There is talking and laughing from the visitors. Jobeni sits with his age group near Ntamo, who shouts to him:]

NTAMO: So, Jobeni, you too are leaving for Johannesburg?

JOBENI: Yes, my lord. I did not think to go quite so soon, but I took a bag of corn on credit from Shorty the trader, and now he says I have joined the mines.

NTAMO: The mines are dangerous.

JOBENI: Yes, but I have been there often before, and know the work.

INDUNA: Are you afraid?

JOBENI: [*laughing*] Oh yes. Each time the cage goes down, all is dark. I think I am dead. But once, when I didn't go to the mines I could only get work on a farm, and that was worse.

HELEMU: I wonder what the Whites do with all the gold we dig for them?

JOBENI: They say that they put it in the bank — but what can it buy in the bank? Oh! They are full of lies!

HELEMU: Yes, they think we are children. Do you know, they tell us that the earth goes round the sun, and that the world is like a ball with water all around. As though it wouldn't spill! And how could we stand and walk if the earth rolled under our feet? We would be moving on our heads!

NTAMO: Wife, fill my bowl again, and give another pot to Jobeni's group.

NABOSIKOVA: I come, my lord.

NTAMO: You have brewed well today, women. Everyone will be merry.

[*As each group finishes a bowl, it praises the host. A Praiser parades up and down, shouting the specific praises of Ntamo.*]

[IN VERNACULAR]   Zwane, Msutu of Solo,
                        Mncuba, son of Tekwane of Puhlapi,
                        You of the mountains,
                        You who roll over small stones.

                        Ntamo, wisdom of councils
                        Whose words have the point of spear,
                        Destroying opposition,
                        Escaping tax.
                        Toothless jaws
                        That crush small beasts,
                        Ntamo of Tekwane of Puhlapi.

NTAMO: Give the Praiser beer. Come, man, let us sing.
    [*he gives the lead – a fine solemn song*]

[IN VERNACULAR]   The hut of spears is empty,
                        The iron is melted, is melted,
                        ZZ   u   ZZ   u

                        The earth is iron,
                        We die, my King, [*repeated*]
                        ZZ   u   ZZ   u

                        The earth is stone,
                        We die, my King. [*repeated*]

                        [*Jobeni rushes out and gives a dance of huge leaps, while he shouts over and over again:*]

                        Catch the bull,
                        Beat it down, Hoosh.
                        [*or other solo-dance song in vernacular*]

[*The men take up the chorus:*]
Beat it down.
[*The women applaud the performance and LaHlope Jnr. shouts:*]

LAHLOPE Jnr: We'll miss you tomorrow when you leave for the other women!

[*Not to be outdone, the women start their own song, and NaboSikova puts on Cocoon anklets that rattle merrily, and dances out, singing, while the women beat time with their hands and join in the chorus.*]

NABOSIKOVA: Beat the rattles.

CHORUS: Little feet jump.

JOBENI: [*rises*] The sun is setting now, and I have much to do before tomorrow. I must say goodbye.

NABOSIKOVA: Yes, my child, and when you see my son tell him the fields are weeded, and the rains have come.

JOBENI: Yes, mother, as soon as I have a day off I will go to him at the address the teacher wrote for me.

[*Exit Bigwapi unostentatiously*]

NABOSIKOVA: May you find him well.

NTAMO: Tell him too, the cow with the white spots is in calf.

LAHLOPE Snr: And don't forget to tell him that his daughter.
Tekani, is growing into a real woman. [*laughter*]

LAHLOPE Jnr: Yes, let him look out for a rich son-in-law.

JOBENI: I will tell him. [*laughing*]

[*Re-enter Bigwapi*]

BIGWAPI: [*shouts with passion*] And give him something from the one all others scorn! [*displays wonderful beaded walking stick*]

NTAMO: [*angrily*] What is that woman saying now?

[*There are exclamations of admiration:* 'What a beautiful stick.' 'What colours.' 'What design.' 'What skill.' *Buzz of talk and Bigwapi crosses to give stick to Jobeni.*]

LAHLOPE Snr: [*bitterly*] So this is what she was doing all the time she was alone. Too sick to come and work with us.

C

LAHLOPE Jnr: I told you she was cunning. Always she tried to steal him from us with words, and potions, and gifts.

NABOSIKOVA: Hush, my daughters, a man wants more than sticks.

END OF SCENE TWO

SCENE THREE

[*The same, a few days later. It is almost dark but for the glow of the late afternoon light. A terrible storm outside, with flashes of lightning. Ntamo, NaboSikova, Bigwapi, Tekani, and Induna.*]

NTAMO: Where are the other Queens now? They should be with us in the hut, protected from the skies. Why have they not returned? Do they not see the black clouds gathering behind the mountains? Many times have I told you that the young one should not wander far.

NABOSIKOVA: Never has she been as late as this. Perhaps she was tired, and rested on the way. I will scold her when she returns.

INDUNA: It is bad that this year we did not peg the home against the lightning.

BIGWAPI: How the wind shrieks. A person in pain could cry like that.

TEKANI: Granny, I'm afraid.

NABOSIKOVA: Sit close to me, child of my child.

BIGWAPI: I think the king is fighting with his mother, and all the royal ancestors are taking part. They say it is the male that sends the lightning and the crackling thunder, and the mother tries to soften him and bring the rain.

NABOSIKOVA: How fearful are the witches who play with lightning and throw it where they want. I remember my mother telling me there was a witch in her husband's home

who wrapped the lightning bird in a cloud no bigger than a
man's hand, and sent it from a clear noon-day sky to strike
her hut. I was only a baby then, and mother had gone outside with me on her back.

BIGWAPI: *Hau!* The ancestors saved you?

NABOSIKOVA: Yes. As the lightning struck there rose a streak
of fire, green like new summer's grass, mixed with blood,
that reached upwards to the mountain top. People from all
around remember the horror.

BIGWAPI: *Hau!*

NABOSIKOVA: There was no wind that day, but that hut burned
so fast that even as my mother ran towards it shouting
'Help,' the last grass crackles and only a hard grey stone —
droppings of the lightning bird — remained!

INDUNA: What did they do?

NABOSIKOVA: [*slowly*] They found out who was the witch.
My father went to the Great Diviner, Butelezi, whose son is
Manchuman of whom they speak today. The ancestors have
hollowed out their heads that they can see all things. Our
home was far from the White men then, and when father
came home he pointed out the witch. Our mothers killed
her with stones, then threw her down the precipice to rot.

NTAMO: It was good. Now the government protects the witches,
and we must suffer. [*sudden crash of thunder, and everyone starts.*] Where can those women be? Induna, get ready
the potsherd with medicine for me to drive the storm from
the home. [*in the background a call,* 'Mother', 'Mother'.]

NTAMO: [*moving out of the hut*] Who is that?

VOICES OFF: It is the women. We are coming.

[*NaboSikova, Ntamo and the Induna go out of the hut while
Bigwapi remains as though uncertain what to do, and
mutters to herself.*]

BIGWAPI: They are back. Nothing could have happened.

[*The others return, half dragging, half carrying the Little
LaHlope.*]

What has happened? What is the matter?

LAHLOPE Snr: Help her. We were on the path near the river when
we saw the clouds, and I said, 'Let us hurry, it is growing
dark.' So we hurried, and then she stumbled — there was no
stone, but still she stumbled, and then she fell. I helped her
up. She is in pain.

NABOSIKOVA: Do not waste time in talking. It is the child. Her
time has come. Get ready the birth hut. This wonder is
not for men and babes. I will take a brand to light the
fire, and will follow you.

LAHLOPE Snr: Come sister, you must be brave — not like those
women who are drunk with sleeping with a man yet cannot
give birth to his child without shameless cries.

LAHLOPE Jnr: I listen. Help me!

BIGWAPI: Do you want me to help?

LAHLOPE Jnr: No, no. Stay behind.

BIGWAPI: I will wait in my hut.

[*Exit the three women, leaving NaboSikova, Tekani, and
the two men.*]

NABOSIKOVA: I do not like this that has happened.

NTAMO: Come, go to your work.

NABOSIKOVA: It should not take long.

[*Lightning, blackout. Voices from the birth hut. LaHlope
Snr. and NaboSikova are happily excited and bawdy as
befits the occasion.*]

Build up the fire. Why must you choose a night like this to
make me work? Come, my grandchild, that I can see you.
What a thing this is. How sweet to bring out life. What!
You wince! Ha! Are you a virgin that you cannot stand
pain?

LAHLOPE Snr: Strengthen yourself, sister. You are a woman
today, or never will be.

LAHLOPE Jnr: Let me have courage. Let it come out well. Let it
be a boy.

NABOSIKOVA: Why did my son give cattle for you? You young

ones are too soft. Let me hold your arms. Help us — we
cannot do it for you — if it doesn't come soon we'll see
with whom you have been playing. Aya! You will tell us
with whom you have been stealing pleasures in the mealie
fields!

LAHLOPE Jnr: Let me rest. I am tired.

LAHLOPE Snr: Do not tire. Strengthen yourself.

NABOSIKOVA: Hold on to me. We are ready. Why are you so
weak? Let it come. I want it. Will it be a boy to drive the
cattle to the fields, or a girl to sweep our huts and cook for
us? It would be good to have a boy — my first grandson.
Let the ancestors hear me.

LAHLOPE Snr: *Hau!* I cannot feel it moving.

NABOSIKOVA: What are you saying! Wake, you lazy thing. Wake!
[*There is a violent flash of lightning and a burst of thunder,
which seems to be followed by pitch darkness. Bigwapi is
seen in the doorway, her blanket over her head for protection.*]

BIGWAPI: Sister.

NABOSIKOVA: [*from within*] Who is there?

BIGWAPI: Me — Bigwapi.

LAHLOPE Jnr: [*shouts*] Send her away!

NABOSIKOVA: What do you want?

BIGWAPI: [*pleads*] Let me help. I do not want to be alone. I am
afraid of the lightning.

LAHLOPE Jnr: Go away! Go away!

BIGWAPI: Mother, let me stay.

LAHLOPE Snr: [*comes out of the hut*] No! Go, go, don't you
see this is her time?!

LAHLOPE Jnr: [*makes a sudden scream*]
[*LaHlope Snr. re-enters the hut.*]

BIGWAPI: [*standing outside the door, speaks slowly, in a voice
full of anguish*] All right — I will go. How gladly would I
have that pain. I would not cry, but shout with joy. That
little wife does not know what suffering is. To watch all
women nurse their babies while my arms are empty. To have

no daughter to work beside me in the fields, no son to eat the cattle of my hut. To have no son's wives to serve me in my old age, no home where I am mother. That is suffering! There is no pain where there is fullness — only when there is nothing, nothing, nothing.

[*Black out*]

NABOSIKOVA: At last!

NABOSIKOVA and LAHLOPE Snr: A boy. A boy.

LAHLOPE Jnr: A boy!

NABOSIKOVA: Wait! It is not finished. Give me the knife [blade from the tall grass] to cut the cord.

LAHLOPE Snr: What is the matter?

LAHLOPE Jnr: Is he all right? Why is he silent?

LAHLOPE Snr: Quiet! He is still a thing — a weak and little thing.

LAHLOPE Jnr: He makes no sound.

NABOSIKOVA: He has no strength. His body is like water. Child, do not go and leave me behind. How much have I thought of you. How long have I waited for a man child for my old age. First one of my only son. Son of Sikova, do not leave me! In my heart I saw you, Oh tiny thing. I saw you grow to manhood — your voice was sweet and your body an assegai in the dance, and still you would come to me for tales of olden times, and on you would I rest, and you would be my strength. Great is the love of a mother for her child, and her child's child is her reward. Her son she teaches. Her son's son she may spoil! Wake! Open your eyes! Cry, baby, cry! It is no use. This is terrible! It is a thing! Its mouth does not open. Its eyes do not see. It is cold. It is dead!

[*lightning in background then silent darkness*]

END OF SCENE THREE

Act 3

SCENE ONE

A room in a Johannesburg township, small, overcrowded, with the usual ugly furniture – table, four chairs, three-piece chesterfield suite in ugly green with shiny wooden arms; dresser with odd bits of china. Stove in recess of room, with pots and pans above it. Calendar and big photographs on the walls. Gramophone blaring latest jazz.

FERDINAND: [*comes in with Sikova in an ill-fitting jacket and grey trousers*] Hiya pals!

ELIAS: How-do, chaps.

FERDINAND: This is the Swazi whom I told you about. He whose eyes are always turned to home.

VOICES: 'Sikova, the Owl!'[24] 'He looks fresh.' 'The chap who doesn't like Joburg,' etc.

ELIAS: Good, let him drink and forget his troubles. Today we've strong stuff in here. [*calls Martha*] Martha!

MARTHA: [*a big buxom woman in an untidy European dress*] Greetings, men. What do you want?

FERDINAND: Here's a bob. Give us KB.[25]
[*Martha goes to a corner of the room, picks up a broken piece of linoleum, dips in a tin, and places it before Ferdinand, who drinks.*]

ELIAS: Well, how is it?

FERDINAND: [*drinking*] *Hau!* It's strong enough! It cracks the pan. Drink, man.

SIKOVA: [*drinks*] *Hau!* It is bitter.

ELIAS: Better give him Tears of the Queen of England. Have you

39

    tasted it yet, boy?

SIKOVA: No, what is it like?

ELIAS: [*with the rapture of a connoisseur*] Tears of the Queen
    of England! The White people call it brandy. It looks like
    golden water, and after half a jack you are sweet all over.

SIKOVA: [*sceptically*] Half a jack. What's that? I am sure it
    would not make *me* sweet all over.

FERDINAND: [*tolerantly*] You're still a sucker. You're still
    beneath the hearth and know nothing.

ELIAS: Have you tasted askokiaan?

SIKOVA: No.

ELIAS: Have you tasted mbamba?

SIKOVA: No.

ELIAS: Have you tasted kill-me-quick?

SIKOVA: Yes, a few days ago. I took one mouthful and didn't
    like it.

    [*laughter from drinkers*]

ELIAS: Well, Tears of the Queen is better than all those put
    together. I mix it with something else too.

SIKOVA: I don't think I want to taste it.

ELIAS: My friend, just wait awhile. Joburg has not yet caught
    you, but it will if you wait. You still long for *tshwala* made
    from the red corn and the white mealies. I pity you. You do
    not rejoice at this place. Your eyes are sad. I know the
    thoughts. They were mine too, once. You would rather
    have mats under your bones than a bed, and hear cattle than
    trams, and wash your body in a running brook than cover
    it with White men's suits. Try this, though, and let me sing
    you the song of Johannesburg.

    [*Elias, Ferdinand and others join, and couples and individuals
    dance in the crowded room. Sikova stands looking on, lost
    and bewildered.*]

        My name is left behind me
        With a Shangaan girl,
        My name is left behind me

With a Zulu girl,
My name is left behind me
With a Tswana girl,
My name is left behind me
With a Tchopi girl as well.
Oh! The loose girls of Johannesburg,
With all of them I left my name!

ELIAS: Here, let me just show what brandy can do for you. How much money have you?

SIKOVA: [*hesitates*] Ten shillings.

ELIAS: All right. I will add my ten bob. You shall have a good drink and be near to heaven quickly.

[*Martha fetches brandy and glasses from behind dresser.*]

FERDINAND: Let him be. *Tshwala* is strong enough for him.

ELIAS: No! It is terrible to have somebody so sad when we are all happy. Martha, bring the brandy. Give me your money, boy.

[*Very reluctantly Sikova counts out ten shillings while Elias elaborately opens the bottle that Martha brings, and pours out a large glass.*]

ELIAS: I will show you how. [*swills it down*] Zz it's good! It hots the back of my head and mixes all the senses.

FERDINAND: [*reprovingly*] Why burn him as we are burnt? He is still a calf. You can't force horns.

ELIAS: [*a little drunkenly*] You are like a granny, Ferdinand. Drink, boy, you are no woman.

[*Sikova takes the tumbler which Elias has refilled, and is about to drink when there is a knock at the door. Elias quickly stands in front of Sikova, and Martha quickly shoves the bottle down her bosom. Others sit, pretending to talk of this and that.*]

ELIAS: Who is there?

JOBENI: Just a person.

ELIAS: [*opens door cautiously, then*] Come in.

JOBENI: [*enters carrying a parcel. Looks round, sees Sikova.*] Sikova! I have found you at last!

SIKOVA: Jobeni! My age mate! How it rejoices me to see you!

JOBENI: Our eyes are old with absence.

SIKOVA: When did you leave home?

JOBENI: Two moons past. I sought you at the address the
teacher wrote for me, but couldn't find you there, and no
one knew where you were. And on the mines you are not
free to visit friends in town. When I get off on Sunday I
must dance. Lots of White people come to look and clap
their hands. They see how fine a dancer I am [*laughs*]. It
was hard to get away to find you.

SIKOVA: Oh! You have had trouble on my account, brother, and
I thank you. I too went first to the address, but my kinsman
whom I sought had disappeared.

FERDINAND: It's like that in Johannesburg, my friend. You
move your hide-out – change your name.

SIKOVA: Oh yes, Jobeni. Here I am called TOM. [*loud laughter*]

ELIAS: Tom – you mean Tomcat! [*laughs*] You should not let
them call you that.

JOBENI: [*ignoring Elias*] So what did you do when your kinsman
wasn't there?

SIKOVA: For days I wandered around. I had my papers with me,
but as you know, I cannot read or speak English. I could
only say, 'Work Missus.' If I had not met this friend,
Ferdinand, I do not know what would have become of me.
This place is frightening for us who know nothing.

ELIAS: [*cheerfully*] True, boys. The Whites teach their dogs to
bark at us when we go into their yards, and the police throw
us into pick-up vans when we run from the dogs!

JOBENI: Then what do you do?

ELIAS: If you're a fool, you try to explain. If you're wise, you
say, 'Yes, *baas*, thank you, *baas.*' They think we are fools,
and they treat us like robbers.

SIKOVA: I do not like the city.

FERDINAND: It is all right, brother, when you are used to it.

JOBENI: What work have you?

SIKOVA: Oh! You would die laughing. Ferdinand took me in
with his boss. I'm the woman in the shop. I sweep and dust,
and scrub floors, like this [*demonstrating with accompanying
noises*] and even wear an apron. But Ferdinand goes on
messages on a bicycle, and knows every street in the whole
city!

FERDINAND: It is my home now, Tom.

JOBENI: Are you a Swazi?

FERDINAND: A Swazi from a White man's farm. I ran away
when I was a boy, but was glad to find a brother in this
place where men are enemies.

JOBENI: [*with dignity*] Thank you for helping my friend. He is
a good man. He is strong, but does not like to fight, and is
always generous. [*to Sikova*] Tell me, have you sent much
money home?

SIKOVA: Of course. Two pounds. And I have bought blankets
for my mother, and will buy some for my wives here, too.
Things are cheaper here than in the stores at home.

JOBENI: You have done well, my friend.

SIKOVA: Tell me things of home.

JOBENI: When I left the fields were weeded, and the black cow
with the white spots was in calf —

SIKOVA: [*interrupting*] And had the little LaHlope had the
child?

JOBENI: No, not yet. But I brought you something from your
wife, Bigwapi. I wrapped it up because I was afraid its
beauty might make even good men thieves.
[*Undoes the parcel containing the stick. The men admire it
greatly.*]

FERDINAND: [*laughing*] How that woman must love you!

SIKOVA: [*Becomes inspired — a new personality as he recalls
Bigwapi to mind, and during his speech he moves to the
centre of the stage, and ends speaking direct to the audience,
unaware of all those in the shebeen.*]
She is most diligent with her hands. Never have I tasted beer

such as hers. She never left me without it. And she can sew
beads more beautifully than any other, with designs so
skilful none can copy them. If she sees a thing but once, she
will remember it and make hers better. The belts and neck-
laces she makes will never come undone, each bead so
perfect in its place. Her thatching too, smooth as the outside of a clay pot, and when she plaits a mat it is more
comfortable and fine than White man's cloth. In the dance,
her shoulders move like the wind beneath still water, and
her hands are like reed fronds. And she is beautiful as the
shining sun, and the unsoiled sands of the sea.

JOBENI: [*in horror*] Brother, brother, stop yourself! Are you
bewitched? Has she sent dream magic to steal your heart in
this way?

FERDINAND: [*very seriously*] Your friend is right, my boy.
Never let a woman, especially one wife amongst others, ride
on your head like that. She can do you harm.

SIKOVA: [*abashed*] Forgive me. I was lonely for things of home.

ELIAS: So, let him drink and forget this nonsense. Let him forget
everything for a while. Martha, what are you up to now?
Come on. Here's my mug, fill it up.

VOICE: Give us a number.

CHORUS: *Ja*, that's the ticket.

[*Jobeni and Sikova sit together on one side.*]

SIKOVA: How do your own affairs go?

JOBENI: Fine. She will wait for me, and you must show her that
you do not want her.

SIKOVA: I will do all I can to help you.

[*gramophone plays* 'Angissena Baba No Mama' (*jive series*),
*cuts out talk between Sikova and Jobeni. People dance. As
the number finishes, a loud knock.*]

ELIAS: Who's there?

POSTMAN: It's only me, Peter, the postman.

ELIAS: Come in.

MARTHA: *Hau*! This time I thought it was the police. [*She takes out bottle with relief.*] But of course, they never knock! What do you want, Peter?

POSTMAN: [*producing letter*] I brough this letter for Sikova Zwane addressed care of Ferdinand, and I knew Ferdinand would be here.

SIKOVA: A letter for me? It is a long time since I heard from home. [*turning to Ferdinand*] My friend, read it to me.

FERDINAND: [*doubtful about opening the letter*] Now? Here?

SIKOVA: Yes, I cannot wait. [*with some embarrassment*] No – I will wait.

ELIAS: Why wait? What can be in such a letter but good greetings from home? [*pompously*] People who cannot write do not send real letters. They must borrow somebody else's hand. It is like the boss who has a secretary whom he can make write all his letters, except his secret ones. You cannot speak your heart through someone else's hand. You are two people, and one is shy of the other. And what comes out is not what you really feel, but only the shadow of the sun. We are friends here, Tom. How can you sit with this letter and not hear it read?

POSTMAN: So much gas about a letter! It makes me dry after all the trouble in finding the owner.

SIKOVA: [*takes the hint, and passes him the still full glass*] Forgive me, postman, I forgot myself. Will you drink this?

POSTMAN: Thank you.

FERDINAND: Who writes for your people of the home, my friend?

SIKOVA: The teacher.

ELIAS: [*triumphantly*] You see!

SIKOVA: Then read it to me, Ferdinand.

FERDINAND: All right, I will read it. [*opens the letter and reads haltingly*] It is from your father – 'My dear son, how is your health? We are sorely troubled. There is illness, terrible illness in the home. Your child is dead. The new child of your little wife. You must return at once.'

SIKOVA: My child, dead! [*with a whisper*] Oh, my father — [*He weeps.*]

ELIAS: [*awkwardly*] Be brave, Tom. [*pours him another glass*]

FERDINAND: I am sorry, my friend.

ELIAS: Drink, it will strengthen you.

> [*Elias forces him to take the glass, and he sits stunned with it in his hand as suddenly the door is burst open and police rush in. There are wild shouts from the Africans, some of whom push past the police, shouting,* 'Cops.' 'Run.' 'Police.' *The police shout,* 'We've got you this time, you bastards.' 'Come on.' Sikova *remains seated as though paralysed, the glass still in his hand. A policeman grabs it from him and shouts,* 'Look at this kaffir — too drunk to move. This will wake you up.' *He strikes Sikova in the face and marches him off.*]

END OF SCENE ONE

SCENE TWO

An open field outside a village. A tree in the background, and blazing sun. Ntamo, Helemu and the Induna are sitting on the ground, waiting.

NTAMO: Now that I have come to our journey's end all my body is with pain.

HELEMU: Have comfort, brother. Your pain will ease when the truth is revealed. You are at present like a pus-swollen wound, the pain of which can only be relieved with a deep cut through which the poison must be spilt. All your hates and fears are suppurating, because they cannot be expressed. We are not women who can brood on pain without revenge. We are strong men and must rout out evil — even with a spear! When you have acted as the Diviner will tell you, the blood in your body will shine again!

INDUNA: Yes, it is not acting, not doing, which confuses the senses so that questions strike like hailstones in the skull. Until we know what we must do, we will go on asking ourselves, 'what can have happened to your son that he sends no word from the Place of Gold? Why does he not return to put a stone upon the grave, and purify himself, and cool the spirit?'

NTAMO: Stop! My head no longer takes well. I have waited long and silently while evil things have broken through my world, so that the paths I tread seem walled with traps through which I blunder. The knowledge of my fathers makes me seek that which I know has already gone. Only the Diviners remain with their great wisdom of things past and still to come — and so I put my trust in this great Manchuman.

HELEMU: He will enlighten us. When we know, we may find peace.

NTAMO: The mother of Sikova told me that the bereaved one cries in her sleep at night, and fights with things we cannot see.

INDUNA: There were droppings of the hyena near the water hole where the cattle went to drink.

HELEMU: The day before we left I heard an owl screeching from a treetop, and as I looked it blinked, and did not move, but even as my eyes were on it, it disappeared into the setting sun without stirring from the tree. We could not stay with all this not knowing. Why did the lightning come that night? Why did she stumble on an unseen stone? We are in darkness.

NTAMO: We are in the darkness of the living and the dead. My fear is also for my son. Did we send him on a road of death when we let him go alone into the City? Would it not have been better had he gone to the mines? Though, never can I forget what happened to my other son. We did not even have his body to bury, but laid his empty clothes within a hole.

They said his body was all broken.

HELEMU: Why do we suffer so? Is the life of all people, suffering?

NTAMO: We suffer so because we stand upon a bridge, and the
one end that was built in rock has broken, and you and I
are too old to reach the other side, and the young are too
foolish to distinguish sand from stone. Oh, that the great
Manchuman may show me the truth that I may find release
from all my doubts in action, and bring back the evil on the
one who struck our hearts with death.

[*Noise of singing in the background. Manchuman enters
from the back – a strange figure in a diviner's outfit. Follow-
ing him are a few disciples chanting a Sangoma song. They
walk forward and take their places near Ntamo and his men.
Manchuman is impressive – a consummate actor believing in his
role and in his occult power.*[26]]

HELEMU: Look, I think he comes!

NTAMO: Of course it is he. You cannot mistake the leader from
the led – the sun from its shadows. May his deep powers
not fail him now.

HELEMU: Do not fear. When spirits such as his enter a man they
show him secrets of all the world, and evil-doers cannot
hide their nakedness from him. His knowledge is as deep as
the entrails of the earth. For days and nights he can remain
in deepest pools, and speak with the spirits of the dead.
When he emerges, snakes caress his chest, and white beads
glisten in his hair. His eyes are blind, and still he sees things
past and to come, like a White man's book in which lies
great wisdom for those who have the secret of the written
word!

[*Manchuman and his disciples advance through the audience
singing, towards the end of this speech.*]

HELEMU: Father, we beg the head.

MANCHUMAN: Leave it. Do not tell me the purpose of your
journey. My spirits will guide me. Ndau.[27]

CHORUS: Ndau.

HELEMU: [*placing money in front of Manchuman*] To open the
    mouth.

MANCHUMAN: It is not enough. Give me another L1.

HELEMU: We do not have it here, when you show the light we
    have two goats at home that we can give you.

MANCHUMAN: [*taking up the money*] This and two goats to
    show the truth. Strike!

CHORUS: Ndau!

MANCHUMAN: [*Inhales snuff and stares at the men as though to
    hypnotise the truth for them.*]

CHORUS: [*Sings in vernacular and claps hands to the rhythm.*]
            Let the spirits see
            And the voices speak.
            All the spirits,
            All the voices,
            Come together here.
  Refrain: Let the spirits see
            And the voices speak.

    [*The song is repeated for a while, then Manchuman puts up
    his hand, breathes hard, gives a high whistle, and says:*]

MANCHUMAN: Silence! [*long pause*] They come. Strike!
    [*Ntamo, Helemu and Chorus shout together 'Ndau!' At the
    same time they flick the left hand so that the fingers make a
    whip-like noise. Manchuman's followers take their cue from
    the supplicants, striking loudly and shouting loudly when the
    supplicants do, and softly when their response is soft, the
    second 'siyavuma' ['we agree'] being the main clue.*]
    You have travelled far. A winding road.

CHORUS: *Siyavuma. Siyavuma.*

MANCHUMAN: From the setting of the sun behind the mountains.

CHORUS: [*loudly*] *Siyavuma, siyavuma.*

MANCHUMAN: Ndau. You were driven by something that you
    greatly feared.
    [*Whistles, and beats his chest with his hands.*]

CHORUS: [*loudly*] *Siyavuma, siyavuma.*

MANCHUMAN: [*bites a bit of wood medicine, and mumbles to himself in broken sentences which seem nonsense.*] There is the earth. Full, they come. What do they eat? Evil dances. [*suddenly breaks out loudly*] The death of a woman.

CHORUS: [*softly*] *Siyavuma. Siyavuma.*

MANCHUMAN: Of a man.

CHORUS: *Siyavuma.*

MANCHUMAN: A man child.

CHORUS: [*excitedly*] *Siyavuma! Siyavuma!*

MANCHUMAN: Yes, you have come about the death of a child. A child not yet strong, not yet running. A twig of a branch. Strike. [*pauses every now and then and inhales hemp. then resumes the drama.*] The child of your child – the first grandson. Killed by a woman of the home!

CHORUS: [*gives huge response*] *Siyavuma! Siyavuma!*

MANCHUMAN: [*off-handedly*] You are bothering me. The bird [*beats his head*] is hitting me. What can I find? Strike.

CHORUS: *Siyavuma. Siyavuma.*

MANCHUMAN: The quarrel is still with the people with whom you eat.

NTAMO: We eat with many people. Who is it?

MANCHUMAN: The person who kills you is a young woman. Before you she has shame.

NTAMO: Who is she? There are many women in my house that show shame before me.

MANCHUMAN: She is not the big wife. She is not the little wife. She stands on the bridge. Waters flow past.

CHORUS: *Siyavuma. Siyavuma.*

NTAMO: [*Almost loses control, and shouts.*] Your head is open. You have hit the road!

MANCHUMAN: [*scoring*] Yes, the body in the middle. Yet it is not liked. [*changing to ordinary voice*] Yes, that is what you must notice. She is a woman with reason for jealousy.

CHORUS: *Siyavuma. Siyavuma.*

MANCHUMAN: It is the child of the first wife whom you must watch.

CHORUS: [*softly*] *Siyavuma.*

MANCHUMAN: [*corrects himself subtly*] That child is still in danger. [*again in a trance*] See the spirits close the path. What do you want? The child of the little wife is eaten. The man child of the little wife.

CHORUS: *Siyavuma. Siyavuma.*

MANCHUMAN: [*grabs his stomach*] Leave me. *Hau, hau.* There is an owl in her grain bin. She sends it out at night. It grabs the stomach. [*makes noises of pain*] Oh, don't eat me.

CHORUS : *Siyavuma. Siyavuma.*

MANCHUMAN: [*dancing about*] The breath went fast, the poison was quick. Her people will deny her witchcraft and blame it on you. They will say, 'Show us our daughter's witchcraft medicine.' It cannot be shown. It is inside. They know it. [*stops abruptly and says in normal clear voice*] Today we are sad. A man-child has gone and witches rejoice!!

CHORUS: *Siyavuma. Siyavuma.*

MANCHUMAN: [*goes into another mood*] Ndau. Smoke. It comes in my head. Where is the thigh? It is far. He is in the city looking for money. He will be foolish when he hears.

CHORUS: *Siyavuma. Siyavuma.*

NTAMO: Indeed.

MANCHUMAN: He will not admit what she has done. He will ask you why. Let me tell you.

CHORUS: [*tensely*] *Siyavuma. Siyavuma.*

MANCHUMAN: [*hits himself, and whistles*] It is womanhood. She wishes to be the big wife.

CHORUS: [*goes flat*] *Siyavuma. Siyavuma.*

MANCHUMAN: She must have a son. She has no son.

CHORUS: *Siyavuma. Siyavuma.*

MANCHUMAN: [*with sudden vision*] She has no son. She has no daughter. [*working to the climax*] She has nothing. She has jealousy because she has never borne — because of her children that have not seen the sunshine. A pumpkin plant without fruit. A branch without flower. That is her darkness.

She is empty!

CHORUS: [*powerfully*] *Siyavuma! Siyavuma!*

NTAMO: Why has she no children? Why?

MANCHUMAN: She has destroyed herself. She is a witch!

NTAMO: Yes, yes. [*While Chorus chants,* 'Siyavuma, Siyavuma.']
And my son? Where is he?

MANCHUMAN: A stone makes ripples on the water before it falls.

HELEMU: Explain further, father.

MANCHUMAN: [*smoking hemp*] Everyone wanders and is lost.
Your son is wandering. He is on a path without end. It is
dark. [*He shakes his head and seems to return to normality.*]
I am tired – give me some snuff. I have done my work. I
have finished. Ndau!
[*Manchuman sits down and his disciples give him snuff, and
then begin to chatter amongst themselves.*]

NTAMO: Now we know. That which we feared, we know! The
spirits showed us that which we feared, and it remains for
me to act. Oh, horrible woman! To destroy the fruit of her
own womb and envy the fruit of others. I will cut her off
like the mealie plant struck with the red blight. But oh my
son, wandering in darkness, why did you choose so wicked
a woman? One who bought her knowledge of evil with the
fruit of her own womb!

HELEMU: I shake when I think of her, and the blood is red
behind my eyes. Tomorrow we will start the long journey
back, and do what must be done.

MANCHUMAN: What will we eat? That which you give me is not
enough.

NTAMO: Here is the light of the road you have shown us. [*gives
him L2*]

MANCHUMAN: [*takes it casually and stuffs it into one of the
little bags*] Don't forget the two goats. There is beer at
home today. Eat before you depart, it is getting late.
[*Exit all. Song for the exit.*]
END OF SCENE TWO

SCENE THREE

Same as Act One. Ntamo, Helemu and NaboSikova.

NTAMO: Mother of Sikova, we have told you all.

NABOSIKOVA: Indeed, my lord, your words have hit me, and
there is nothing I can say. Ants walk in my ears.

NTAMO: When outsiders strike a home revenge is easy. Like war
it has a pleasure all its own, and though the spear that kills
is stained with blood, it can be cleaned and used again. But
it is only pain when the enemy is one who tilled the fields
with you, and reaped your grain, and shared with you the
common pot, and called you 'kinsman'.

HELEMU: A daughter-in-law is always an outsider, my brother, and
can soon become an enemy. She is not of us. She enters
marriage with tears, and never can forget that her own
ancestors are at her parents' home and that here she keeps
their name separate from our own.

NABOSIKOVA: [*bitterly*] It is true, brother-in-law. We women
never forget that at our husband's home we are the strangers,
and only when we are old, so old that blood no longer runs
in our bodies, are we accepted there. Then we control the
young wives of our sons, and watch them suffer too, as we
as young wives suffered. With them we are free until we die,
when we are honoured to have our graves within the cattle
byres we never in life were allowed to enter.

NTAMO: Silence woman! Would you change the law?

NABOSIKOVA: No, my lord [*smiling*]. I am old now and it is
my turn to rule the wives of my sons. But sometimes even
that is hard.

HELEMU: It is the fault of you women, always with tongue.
What are you going to do, my brother, with her that is the
cause of your trouble?

NTAMO: To do? Not what I would like to do, but what I can.

The world is upside down these days when witches flourish
and we who would smell them out are hanged by White men.
I would like to do as our fathers would have done, and call
a meeting in the sun and summon all the people. I would
have them sit naked with their legs stretched out, unable to
hide their horns of poison. The Diviner would dance before
them and strike the guilty with his Hippohide whip that all
might see their shame. Then they would writhe like worms
or snakes, and with their mouths describe how they acted,
by what means they stole the life. If they did not die before
those who watched with eyes of fear, they would be beaten
to death, or thrown down the cliff, or in the dark night the
regiments would surround their huts and burn them to the
ground. Then they and their spawn could never again do
evil on the earth. But now I am bound — bound by the
White man's law.

HELEMU: Indeed, things are not well these days. No-one should
blame us for her death. Instead, we should be praised for
removing from the world a thing of filth, a spring of evil.
But as you say, we would be brought before the White man's
court and while she strumpeted her evil we would be hanged
for naming it. And yet, you must do something, for if she
remains here she will feed on her success and seek other
victims. Do not forget the words of Manchuman — there is
another child that is still in danger.

NTAMO: Yes, I must act quickly.

NABOSIKOVA: Will you not wait until your son returns?

NTAMO: Until she has killed us all? Her tongue of poisoned
sweetness must not deceive us and turn us from our purpose.
[*Enter Bigwapi with a bowl of beer*]
What do you want?

BIGWAPI: I have come with beer to welcome father home.
[*Bigwapi kneels with the bowl, strains it, tastes a little and
hands bowl to Ntamo*]

NTAMO: My mouth is dry, and yet I cannot drink that beer. It is bitter as the aloe that we put upon the brow of corpses. Oh! This deceit that pushes claws into my eyes to make me blind.

NABOSIKOVA: I know not what to say.

HELEMU: Tell her now brother. [*long pause*]

BIGWAPI: What father? Why do you all look at me with eyes of glass? Why, when I greeted you, were you silent? And when I gave you food did your throat refuse to swallow. What have I done?

NTAMO: Oh! wicked thing! As if you did not know. Look in your heart and see what you have done within its darkness You and your fellows, who steal the souls of new born babes, and feast on them, and gloat. Go, tie your bundle. Take the mats on which your body lay, your wooden pillow and your blankets, and the clothes you wear. Return with your baggage to your father's home. I will tell him that we do not want his daughter here. He may keep the cattle we gave for you, in hope of better things, that he may see how much we hate. This will I tell the Chief, and give reasons which we cannot bring into the light.

BIGWAPI: What reasons, father, for this disgrace? What tongues have slandered me? I am no Thing to be thrown back and forth.

NTAMO: Do not talk thus. Would I believe in evil that I did not see with my own eyes? Go. Oh, my ancestors, let me control myself and send her forth with bones unbroken.

NABOSIKOVA: Girl, go quickly.

BIGWAPI: [*defiantly, but with dignity*] I will go, and I will stay at my own home until my husband's return. Then I will speak, and we shall see who has the truth and who lies.

NTAMO: You witch! Do you say that my son will stand against his father? That he will put you in his armpit when I have driven you away, and share his sleeping mat with one who has destroyed the fruits of his manhood? That he will lie with a woman who has never given him a child because she knows it would be a monster?

BIGWAPI: [*sobbing, and horrified*] You lie! You lie! You will
see when I come back.

NTAMO: Never come back [*Exit Bigwapi*]

HELEMU: Each word shouted her wickedness.

NTAMO: May I never see her again. We must have the home
cleansed when she has gone. You are silent, mother of
Sikova?

NABOSIKOVA: I listen, my lord. You spoke justly. She brought
poison into our home and killed the quietness. But it is
hard to send a woman, once married, back to her father's
home to be despised as a thing of nothing. Though she is
young no other man will take her as his wife, and though
her beauty calls him, he must withdraw with dread. As a
woman I speak now, not as a mother. The law of our people
is hard on women.

NTAMO: Are you trying to defend her? To excuse her? The
animal! Come, brother, we must report this matter to the
Chief.

HELEMU: Farewell, mother of Sikova.

NABOSIKOVA: Go well, my lords. [*Alone*] How hard it is. Oh!
my son, when will you return? I know you love her and I
pity her. She is pushed by her heart. Is there any woman
who is not jealous of her co-wives? [*Fearfully*] I must be
quiet.

END OF ACT THREE

Act 4

SCENE ONE

The Shebeen. Elias is lolling on a chair, smoking. Martha, in a corner, is wiping some cups.

ELIAS: These damn raids waste too much. The police aren't human to throw good drink down the drain!

MARTHA: Don't worry. I've got them oiled all right, so you're quite safe for a while.

ELIAS: Fine. That Swazi from the mine is coming again today to see if Ferdinand found his pal.

MARTHA: I wonder what could have happened to that young one. I felt really sorry for him caught with a glass stuck in his hand.

ELIAS: It served him right. The fool sat there like a block of wood. Ferdinand thinks that when he got to the charge office he couldn't even give his name, and that is why he hasn't been able to find him to pay his fine.

MARTHA: He can't have got more than a couple of months. He should soon be out.

ELIAS: *Ja!* And he'll be a wiser and tougher guy.
[*Knock at the door*]
Come in!
[*Enter Ferdinand followed by Sikova who looks shrunken, sullen and furtive. His head has been shaved.*]

FERDINAND: Hullo folks!

ELIAS & MARTHA: Hullo, Ferdinand.

ELIAS: Hullo, Tom. So we've found you at last. Where have you been all this time? How did you like the taste of 'tronk'?[28]

The free food from the Government hasn't made you fat,
has it?

MARTHA: [*sympathetically*] He's thin as a winter leaf.

[*Sikova has taken no notice of Elias and his question, and
has sat huddled on a chair in the corner, in the background.
Elias turns to Ferdinand*]

ELIAS: Where did you find him in the end?

FERDINAND: They'd sent him to Roodepoort, to a road gang,
and they didn't even want to release him when I paid his
money. [*laughing*] I tell you, it was damn hard to find him.

[*Knock at the door. Enter Jobeni, who does not at first see
Sikova.*]

JOBENI: Greetings! Have you found him?

FERDINAND: Yes, there he is.

[*Jobeni goes to him with a smile of welcome.*]

JOBENI: *Hau!* I didn't see you.

[*Sikova looks up, but says nothing, and the words freeze
on Jobeni's lips.*]

[*awkwardly*] How is it, my brother?

SIKOVA: [*dully*] So!

JOBENI: It is good to see you out. I have been disappointed so
often at not finding you here, that today I scarcely hoped.
Why did it take so long to find you?

SIKOVA: [*to Ferdinand, wearily*] You explain.

FERDINAND: It's a long story. As you know, I asked for him
first as Tom, Tom Zwane, and they said, 'Not here'. So the
next time I asked for Sikova Zwane, but that name was not
in the books either. But yesterday I had an idea [*chuckles*].
He has another name still!!

ELIAS: Another name? Did they not ask for your right name?

SIKOVA: [*slowly*] They asked me my name, and I answered 'Tom'.
They shouted, 'Tom what?'. And I said 'Sikova'.

FERDINAND: They wrote him down as Tom Sikova.

ELIAS: Tom Sikova! Tom, the owl. Oh! This is a good joke. Ha,
ha!

SIKOVA: [*suddenly roused*] Stop, you dog of the city! Stop!
    Stop laughing at me!

ELIAS: *Hau,* I hit him then. The bull has woken!

JOBENI: Do not listen to him, my friend.

FERDINAND: Shut up, Elias. Don't notice him, Sikova. Remember,
    he is of the town and has been tied up himself for all his
    cleverness.

SIKOVA: Forgive me, I am confused.

JOBENI: I brought you the stick.

    [*For the first time Sikova's face lights up, and he sits
    straight. He unwraps the stick carefully.*]

SIKOVA: The stick. I thought the police had stolen it.

ELIAS: That's a good one, too. The police have got enough sticks.
    They want heads. They don't get promotion on sticks!!!

SIKOVA: [*half to himself, holding the stick in front of him*] It is
    beautiful and strong. It will help me to my home.

JOBENI: Are you returning?

SIKOVA: Yes.

FERDINAND: I've already told him that I will try to push out
    the boy who took his job, but he won't listen.

SIKOVA: [*dully*] I must be cleansed, and put a stone on my
    child's grave. [*with sudden passion*] I hate the city! I came
    to it for money, only for money. I did no evil to it. I wanted
    to love it. The men of home who had been to it before lied.
    They told of the lights, and food, and wonders you buy for
    a penny. All lies! They did not tell of fear, loneliness, and
    poison. You too, Jobeni, you also lied!

JOBENI: [*shamefacedly*] When I tried to tell you the truth you
    would not listen.

FERDINAND: It is not the city, brother. The city is fine, if it is
    your home.

JOBENI: The city can never be a home.

ELIAS: [*impatiently*] Let him return to his valley and his cows.

JOBENI: Go back, my brother, to our home, that your heart may
    be cooled, and the darkness be wiped away.

SIKOVA: I will seek out the witch who sent me all those sorrows, and take my revenge.

ELIAS: You fellows blame everything on witchcraft! It makes you stupid. Witches may have killed your child, but it was your own greenness which let the police catch you with the dope in your hand. Do you know that there are women in this place who think that witches steal the profit from their beer, so they spend all their profit trying to protect themselves. Martha and I don't do that. Our heads are opened. We buy the cops instead. We don't throw away our money on all this witchcraft nonsense.

MARTHA: [*fearfully*] Quiet, Elias. Don't speak like that. How do you know witches aren't listening to you. I could tell you stories about them all right. . .

FERDINAND: [*interrupting*] Rather give us a drink. This man must soon return to the mines.

JOBENI: [*laughing*] Yes. Now, instead of rushing out to see if you are found, I shall be able to spend my free time dancing in the Compound.

SIKOVA: Ferdinand has told me how you helped me. I don't know when I can give you back the money you paid out.

JOBENI: It can wait. Now that you are returning, greet the people of our home. Tell them I remember them. Tell them that in the mine when I am free, I sing the songs of home, and beat up the dust in the dances they know.
[*During this conversation Ferdinand moves away and begins talking quietly to Elias.*]

SIKOVA: Did you write to my father of my imprisonment?

JOBENI: No, I thought to myself, why tell him you were lost until you were found? In a letter I received from home I saw he already had troubles enough and was working his own way to end them. [*drops his voice*] Who do you think is the witch?

SIKOVA: Do you, too, mock me? Can I divine? In my thoughts I have searched, and found no one. There is no one at home whom I hated. No one at home whom I thought hated me.

Who then desires to destroy me?

JOBENI: [*uneasily*] I cannot say. Your father may. From him
you will find out this secret truth, and it will be hard and
bitter. Diviners think they seek it out, but sometimes they,
too, deceive.

SIKOVA: What secret truth? Are you trying to tell me something?

JOBENI: Nothing, nothing. I want to help you. Why not wait
until I can return with you? We'll find a medicine man here,
and you'll get back your job and earn real money.

SIKOVA: No. I know you are my friend, but I am not alone at
home. My father will help me.

JOBENI: As you wish. I am sorry you will not wait, but I can see
your reason. There is one big thing you shall do for me. Tell
that girl, Lomusa, I do not forget her! No matter what
happens I want her. The cattle will go to her father when I
return. Remember. No matter what happens, I want her. I
trust you.

SIKOVA: [*Impatiently*] Do not worry about that. Though I
have not the money which I sought, I will never touch that
girl. All I seek is the quiet of the home as I remember it.

JOBENI: Perhaps, when the medicine men have made you right,
you will come back to earn the money that you need?

SIKOVA: Never! As long as I have manhood I will try not to
come to the city, but work my fields and earn pennies near
my home.

[*Elias saunters up to them with a drink, and says:*]

ELIAS: The trouble with you is that you came to the city too
late. You are old bones and can't be twisted! [*hands tin to
Jobeni*]. Ferdinand has bought this for you. Do not fear —
today you are safe.

[*Jobeni takes the tin*]

JOBENI: *Nkosi!* [*Drinks, and offers it to Sikova.*]

SIKOVA: [*Shaking his head in refusal*] I thank you, my friend, I
will drink at home when I have bitten the medicine to wipe
away my darkness.

END OF SCENE ONE

SCENE TWO

*The Village, a few days later. Sikova, Ntamo, NaboSikova. Sikova
is still in his ragged town clothes.*

NABOSIKOVA: [*tenderly*] Let me kiss your hand again, my
 son. How thin you have grown. You look tired.

SIKOVA: Yes, mother, there is deep tiredness within. I've longed
 too much for home. Days and nights were long, and full of
 fear after I heard of my baby's death.

NTAMO: My son, why did you not write when your received the
 letter? Did you find a doctor to purify you of the darkness?
 You know it can bring madness on a man not to mourn his
 child with medicine laid down by the custom of our people.
 Why do you look so wild?

SIKOVA: Father, I had no doctor. I had no medicines.

NTAMO: [*horror-stricken*] Why? What did you do?

SIKOVA: Nothing. [*breaks down*] I was in prison.

NTAMO &
NABOSIKOVA: In prison!

SIKOVA: Yes.

NTAMO: What had you done?

SIKOVA: I had done nothing. We were sitting in a house, drinking.
 They made me drink some White man's drink after your
 letter came. I was sitting in the house with friends, and the
 police came in and grabbed me.

NABOSIKOVA: My son, you are in danger, terrible danger. To be
 put in prison the day you heard that your son had died. Oh!
 who wanted to kill you?

SIKOVA: I do not know, but all the time I was in prison my head
 went round, and at night I could not sleep. Someone in my
 cell hit me because I screamed in my dreams. Look at the
 scars!

NTAMO: Did you have no friends to help you?

SIKOVA: Yes. They looked for me to pay my fine, but when I

went to prison and I was asked my name I gave the name I took in town and mixed it with my own, and when my friends came and asked for me by the name of Tom, they were told I was not there. There were too many Toms.

NABOSIKOVA: Did not Jobeni look for you?

SIKOVA: Yes, and it was Jobeni who paid two pounds remaining on my fine, and gave me money to bring me home.

NABOSIKOVA: [*gratefully*] He helped you indeed.

SIKOVA: He is a true friend, and there were other good men in the city. But in gaol were some who should never walk in the sun, nor touch a human being. [*He breaks down again.*] Oh, my father, hell is not under the ground. Prison is hell!

NABOSIKOVA: Could you get no one to write to us for you?

SIKOVA: I do not know. Too great was my trouble, and my shame.

NTAMO: It is no shame to be put into prison for drinking. That is the White man's law against us. You should have thought of the danger to your own health. The dead call the living whom they know and whom they love.

SIKOVA: How bare the homestead looks. Where are my Queens?

NABOSIKOVA: The mother of Tekani and the little wife are in the fields. I sent Tekani to fetch them home, but gave no reason why I wanted them. My eyes are sore with weeping, and I would like to look on their surprise and joy at seeing you return.

SIKOVA: And the other?

[*NaboSikova remains silent, and Sikova looks at his father.*]

NTAMO: Did not Jobeni tell you?

SIKOVA: Jobeni! What did he know?

NTAMO: My son, she is no longer here.

SIKOVA: Not here? Where then? When I passed her hut coming direct to you a coldness struck my chest. It seemed her huts were empty and that the thatch was jagged — though she always kept it neatly trimmed and bound with finest rope. And there was dirt within the yard, which before was swept

and smeared each day. And no fire burned to cook the pots
of food. I thought it was her loneliness that made her not
bother with things I could not see. Mother, what has happened'

NABOSIKOVA: If only I could speak, but all my words seem
choked within my throat.

NTAMO: We drove her out! It was necessary. It was she who
killed your child!

SIKOVA: Bigwapi? The witch who killed my child? Who told you
this?

NTAMO: The Diviners. My brother, Helemu, and I sought them
out, ending at the home of the great Manchuman, who
knows things we cannot see. He pointed out the truth, and
warned that there were others she might strike through that
foul power possessed only by witches. What could I do but
send her home? I did not kill her, though it would have
been the better way.

SIKOVA: I cannot believe it. Bigwapi is no witch.

NTAMO: My son, it is her witchcraft that blinded you. Do not
contradict those chosen by the ancestors to save us.

SIKOVA: Are you sure they pointed out Bigwapi?

NTAMO: That one alone. We had suspected it — they told us
straight.

SIKOVA: Oh great ones, help me! What shall I do? In the City I
vowed that I myself would seek out the murderer of my
son and avenge myself. The home of which I dreamed has
turned into a grave.

NABOSIKOVA: Yes, my child. Since you left, it has become a
place of bitter tears.

SIKOVA: And Jobeni knew. It was that he tried to tell me when
he said 'the secret truth is bitter'. And that, knowing all, he
still wants her sister. I see it now — he said 'Tell her I want
her, no matter what happens'.

NTAMO: Jobeni is a fool. The whole family may be tainted.

SIKOVA: But why should she do it? Tell me, why should she
annihilate me?

NABOSIKOVA: Because she was jealous. She knows that a man
does not want to waste himself, that in the end he will turn
to women who will bear for him.
[*Sudden hubbub outside, and the three wives come in,
shouting at each other.*]

LAHLOPE Snr: Mother, she has returned to kill me and our child!
She met Tekani come to call us home, and spoke to her,
and in her innocence my child replied. I am afraid of that
woman! Afraid of her. She can steal the soul through the
voice.

NABOSIKOVA: Is that the welcome that you give your husband?
[*The wives shout together:* 'My husband', 'Returned?'.
'Let us look at him'.]

LAHLOPE Jnr: [*turns viciously on Bigwapi*] Go away, you
murderer of his child! Do not look on him with those
longing eyes!

BIGWAPI: My husband, help me . . . take me back. Drive off these
women with their lies.

LAHLOPE Jnr: [*wildly*] I will kill you if he takes you back,
though I hang for it. [*attacks Bigwapi*] Help me, my sister.
Hau! She is a mad dog that bites!
[*The women struggle.*]

NABOSIKOVA
& THE MEN: [*shout*] Leave off!

SIKOVA: [*shouts*] Pull them off! Pull them off or they will kill
her!

NTAMO: Stop! All of you!

BIGWAPI: How can you, my husband, let them do this with me?

SIKOVA: They say you killed my child.

BIGWAPI: And you listen to them? Do you not see how they hate
me because you show me love?

LAHLOPE Jnr: You lie! *You* hate *us* because you have no child,
and so, took mine. How did you know our husband had
returned?

NTAMO: Women, be still! Let me question her. What were you

doing near our home? Had I not sent you to your folk?

BIGWAPI: Yes, but I came this morning to weed my fields. I had worked in them for him.

NTAMO: You had no right to touch my soil. We do not want your hand upon our food. Did the people of your home know what you were doing?

BIGWAPI: Why should they stop me? I had heard that everything I had planted, everything I had cared for since he left, was choked with weeds. I left my home before the dawn. I went only to the river garden. I thought no one would see me. Perhaps the ancestors willed otherwise. [*turning to Sikova*] Take me back!

NTAMO: Never will he take you back!

BIGWAPI: Speak for me, my husband. Where will I go? Do not abandon me. Do not turn away your eyes. Oh! You shall suffer as you make me suffer now.

LAHLOPE Snr: Hear how she curses. Her words have the power of evil.

NTAMO: Do you think that a son of mine would cast me off for you? Would choose you above his parents? You, an empty nothing? Above his goodly wives? Is it not clear that we were right — that she is poison? I will strike you to the ground!

[*He raises his stick.*]

SIKOVA: Father, stop! Do not strike her! [*grabs Ntamo's arm*]

NTAMO: Do not interfere with me!

NABOSIKOVA: My son, hold yourself.

SIKOVA: [*shocked at his unfilial behaviour*] Go, Bigwapi! Through you I raised my hand against my father. Never can I take you back. There is too much sorrow all round. But I, too, cannot now remain. I will cleanse myself of that which has been, and then return to the city. It is easier to have enemies that are strangers than to have such sorrow and hate in the home.

NABOSIKOVA: My son, do not leave us again! The town will

destroy you!

LAHLOPE Snr: Do not let her drive you away from us! Are we
nothing?

BIGWAPI: Take me with you! I will work for you. That is all I
ask. All I want.

NTAMO: Hear her — driving him to the city!

BIGWAPI: Let me hear him speak!

NTAMO: Speak! Show her I am your father.

SIKOVA: [*very slowly*] He is my father, and I am going from him.
There is no longer rest beneath his armpit. But I cannot
take you with me. My roots are here, and when I pull them
up I go alone. I do not understand the city, and in it I
would lose you too. But here I no longer feel I have a home.
I no longer see the truth. Before me are things unknown. But
here, what I know has destroyed me. I have lost my manhood. Let me lose myself in the city. Let me be nothing, too.

BIGWAPI: Go alone then. I will not follow. You have exiled
yourself, but I will not forget you. I will not want to forget.
And you, also, will not forget, though you try with the
strength of man. I will be with you in your fears and your
loneliness, and you will remember me in everything you
desire. My words will pursue you, and the memory of the
things we did together, for I am your home. But because
you do not see these things you are running away to the
city alone.

[*Sikova staggers off.*]

LAHLOPE Snr: Where does she find those words, and these deep
thoughts, while we stand dumb?

NTAMO: Go, women, to your work.

LAHLOPE Snr: She has driven him from us.

LAHLOPE Jnr: We have lost him.

NABOSIKOVA: He has lost himself.

LAHLOPE Jnr: She has stolen him from us.

NTAMO: Stop all this! Go now! You have said enough!

[*Ntamo and the two LaHlopes go off, weeping. Bigwapi and*

NaboSikova remain alone.]

BIGWAPI: [*Last appeal*] Mother, pity me. I swear by my father I used no witchcraft. Can you not help me?

NABOSIKOVA: My child, I pity you, but for you there is no help.

BIGWAPI: [*passionately*] The Diviner was right. I am a witch! In my heart.

[*Bigwapi goes off leaving NaboSikova alone on the stage as it gradually darkens.*]

NABOSIKOVA: My child, that is the case with every woman!

END

NOTES

1. The principles of the system of Swazi nomenclature are different from those of modern English usage. The Swazi have (1) several personal names, one given at birth, others acquired later, for example on joining an age-regiment or for some personal achievement. Most personal names have a definite reference to a characteristic or an event, e.g., Lomusa is 'kindness', Bigwapi means 'Where does one report?' and the person is able to explain the origin of these names. (2) A clan name (*sibongo*) inherited in the patrilineal line and comparable to a surname but more inclusive. (3) Extensions of the clan name (*sinanatelo*), which are used in praising a person in terms of clan origin and affiliation. It is considered extremely disrespectful for a younger person to address an older by the personal name, though the reverse is permitted; the clan name is the more usual. (4) A woman on marriage (a) retains her clan name, to which the prefix, La-, is added, or (b) if her father is a prominent man, she may be known by his personal name to which the prefix, La-, is added, or (c) she may be named and addressed by the name of her child with the prefix, Nabo-. In the play both Zwane and Hlope are clan names, hence Ntamo, his sons and his brothers are all Zwane. The two Hlope wives of Sikova Zwane are described as LaHlope, senior and junior. Ntamo's wife is never addressed by his clan name, but is generally courteously addressed as 'mother of Sikova.' For dramatic purposes I have deliberately not given Bigwapi any clan name, and of course Lomusa, her sister, belongs to the same clan.

2. The terms here, 'big wife' and 'little wife', are the equivalent of senior and junior. When two sisters are married to the same man, the younger one is the 'little' or junior co-wife.

3. According to Swazi law, a woman could be sent back if she was barren and the bridewealth would have to be returned (see Introduction).

4. When an important headman dies his main heir should keep the old family homesteads going by placing his own wives at sites perpetuating the old homestead names.

5. *Induna* is the term for a number of officials. In this context *induna* is a councillor. *Nkosi* means 'chief' or 'lord' or any superior. It is also used as a general form of polite address, and the recipient of a gift can acknowledge the donor by saying *Nkosi* before his clan name together with any extensions.

6. *Induna* is the descriptive form and *nduna* the title used in address.

7. It is polite for the donor to belittle a gift, and to talk of an ox as a chicken when providing somebody important with a feast.

8. A Swazi baby is carried on its mother's back in a special sling. The first of these carrying slings is to be provided by the girl's parents from a goat killed specially for her.

9. See Note 5.

10. *Hau, bantu* is a common expression for emotions of pity, admiration or astonishment. The literal translation is, 'oh, people'.

NOTES

11. 'Mother' is a general term of respect. For discussion of the importance of the mother, see Introduction.

12. *Mlamu* is a kinship term for a preferential mate, such as a wife's younger sister. It is a reciprocal term and indicates an easy familiarity in the relationship. For full discussion see my article, 'Kinship Among the Swazi', in *African Systems of Kinship and Marriage*, editors, A. R. Radcliffe-Brown and Daryll Forde, 1950, Pages 86–110.

13. *Mahiya* are shop-bought prints which are, however, worn in a distinctive national style.

14. 'Under four eyes' is a literal translation of a Swazi idiom meaning 'only two people', meeting privately.

15. 'Goli' is the common term for Johannesburg.

16. The Swazi idiom means 'forgive me for interrupting you while you are speaking.'

17. Under colonial rule every Swazi male over the age of 18 years had to pay poll tax and an additional tax for each wife up to the first four.

18. Under Swazi customary law a man is a minor as long as his father is alive and he is not free to dispose of property or money even if he has earned it himself.

19. A euphemism for a woman having children by a lover while the husband is away. Because of the marriage cattle the legal husband is entitled to claim the children as his own if he wishes.

20. 'A bob' is slang for an English shilling.

21. *Tot siens* is a common Afrikaans expression meaning 'see you again soon.'

22. 'We see you' is the customary greeting, equivalent to 'good morning'.

23. The king and his mother are famous as rainmakers throughout the country.

24. *Sikova* is the Swazi word for an owl.

25. 'KB' is the so-called 'Kaffir beer', the name given to the African beer made from sprouted millet and corn. In Johannesburg, Africans were prohibited from buying hard liquor or brewing their own beer with the result that there was an extensive trade in illicit liquor-buying and also the brewing of all sorts of intoxicating potions, such as *skokiaan*, *mbamba* and *kill-me-quick*, which took less time to brew and had quicker effects than *tshwala*, the traditional beer. Police raids were frequent and every year thousands of Africans were imprisoned under the discriminatory liquor laws of South Africa.

26. A diviner (*sangoma*) undergoes a long period of initiation and cannot be dismissed as a quack or a charlatan. His motives and his importance are indicated in the Introduction.

27. The Ndau are a non-Swazi people, well-known for their occult power, and it is believed that one of them may possess a chosen individual and guide him in divination.

28. *Tronk* is the Afrikaans word for gaol and more commonly used by Africans in the towns, who associate gaol with the Afrikaans-speaking police.